The Ever-Transcending Spirit

The Ever-Transcending Spirit

✦

The Psychology of Human Relationships, Consciousness, and Development

Toru Sato

iUniverse, Inc.
New York Lincoln Shanghai

The Ever-Transcending Spirit

The Psychology of Human Relationships, Consciousness, and Development

iUniverse, Inc.

For information address:
iUniverse, Inc.
2021 Pine Lake Road, Suite 100
Lincoln, NE 68512
www.iuniverse.com

Illustration on cover by Yoshiko Sato

ISBN: 0-595-29004-3

Printed in the United States of America

Dear Readers,

This book is dedicated to Yoshiko, my teacher, and partner of life

"So close your eyes for that's a lovely way to be
Aware of things your heart alone was meant to see
The fundamental loneliness goes whenever two can dream a dream together"
(From the song "Wave" by Antonio Carlos Jobim)

Contents

List of Illustrations

Preface

Growing up, listening, reading, and experiencing many things throughout my life, I was exposed to many theories, ideas, and stories to help me understand my everyday existence. Most of these theories were extremely insightful and have been instrumental in developing my understanding of things. As wonderful as they were, these ideas and theories were either only applicable to a limited set of experiences or extremely complex and beyond my comprehension abilities. This dissatisfaction has driven me to search, integrate, and create a simple theory to explain as much of our experiences as possible. Due to this wonderful opportunity to learn these theories and ideas as well as experience this dissatisfaction, I feel I have been somewhat successful in this endeavor for a relatively simple unified theory.

Some of you may be familiar with my first book, "Rhythm, Relationships, and Transcendence: Patterns in the Complex Web of Life". The present book is in many ways a revision of some parts of that book including many of the discoveries I have made since the time that first book was written. I have tried to make the present book more organized, concise, and reader friendly than the former book. As you read this, please keep in mind that this is only one way to understand our experiences among many. It is not the right way or a better way. There is a proverb by the Blackfoot native tribe in North America that translates, "There are many paths to a meaningful sense of the natural world." Thus, I suggest these ideas put forth in this book not as dogma, but as a possible path and a theory in progress. While we are looking at the big picture, I would also like to mention that, like any organism, my understanding of things is in continual progress. Although I hope that my understanding will develop beyond what it is now, I would like to introduce my present understanding of things at this point in my life. Therefore, my views may change in the future as I expose myself to new and more wonderful experiences and ideas.

I have tried to structure this book so that one section leads naturally into the next section. Some of these sections assume that the reader understands what has been discussed in the previous sections. By adding bits and pieces to the understanding already established from the previous sections, I am hoping that many readers enjoy progressing through the book smoothly. Due to this structure, however, some readers may find some parts of this book overly simplistic and others may find other parts of the book overly theoretical. Furthermore, many readers may also find various parts of this book to overlap in content since all of the ideas discussed in the book relate to each other in many ways. To some extent, the overlap is useful to illustrate the relationships among the various ideas and to discuss certain things from a variety of vantage points. However I understand that those readers who are well versed on this topic may find certain parts of the book repetitive for this reason. I apologize for this inconvenience since I have yet to figure out a way around this problem while still conveying my message to a wide range of readers.

Lastly I would like to mention that what I am about to explain is not completely new and original. The ideas discussed in this book may most adequately be considered as a unique interpretation and integration of what many other individuals have mentioned in many different ways. Thus, I am extremely grateful for the many individuals who have contributed to my understanding of what is written in this book. Some of these individuals are well-known writers/scholars whose works I am only beginning to understand and others are family members and friends who have shared important insights through their everyday behaviors and attitudes as well as the conversations I have had with them. Although there are too many to mention, I am extremely grateful to all of these extraordinary individuals. I would, however, like to mention one very special person I would like to thank. I would like to thank Yoshiko Sato for creating the illustration on the cover and helping me create the figures in this book. Most importantly though, I thank her for inspiring me to learn about the many things that make life so extraordinary and beautiful.

Human Communication

The Universal Language

Having grown up in a variety of cultures, one of the things that fascinated me the most was how despite the differences among people in cultures, people are people. I was especially fascinated by the fact that even if two people do not speak a word of the same language, they are able to communicate with each other to some extent. This is also evident when we communicate with animals that do not understand our language. From these experiences, it was obvious to me that there are two channels of communication. One channel is verbal. The verbal channel is very useful in communicating information about the outside world. This is very effective when the people communicating use the same language. The other is the non-verbal channel. This channel is very effective in communicating about the nature of our relationship with the person (or animal) we are interacting with. This does not require the people communicating to use the same language. Although the verbal channel is easily observable and commonly discussed among many communication experts, the non-verbal channel is a little trickier. Let's examine this tricky channel in a little more detail.

Many scholars throughout history have pointed out that there are numerous universals in **emotional expression** and **non-verbal communication** (e.g., Mesquita & Frijda, 1992; Wilson, 1998). For example, **physical contact** is used as a form of greeting and a gesture of intimacy in all cultures. As a general rule, the more intimate the relationship, the more we touch. Strangers of the same sex typically touch on the arms only. As familiarity with the other person increases, the area of the body that is in contact as well as the frequency of contact increases. This increase is exaggerated for intimate people of the opposite sex. Another good example would be the non-verbal expressions we make with our **eyes**. Although our pupils sometimes dilate in situations of great danger, dilation of pupils is more commonly perceived as a positive response to others in interpersonal situations. In contrast, closing our eyes and wrinkling our nose is a universal sign of disgust and rejection. In addition, these non-verbal forms of communication occur more prominently with women than with men in almost all cultures.

1

The **mouth** is another part of the body we commonly use to send universal non-verbal signals. For instance, pushing our tongue out and spitting are aggressive displays of contempt and rejection. Moreover, pulling down both ends of our mouths and exposing our lower teeth is often a sign of threat and contempt. In contrast, licking our lips is a common sign for appetite, social or otherwise. In an interpersonal context, it is a sign for social invitation used most commonly during flirtation. Finally, as we all know, a **smile** has its characteristic features in the eyes and mouth. It is a universal signal of joy, love, and acceptance.

Although there is some variation in the details, the very basic forms of non-verbal communication seem to be universal. If we examine human communication even further, we discover that these commonalities of non-verbal communication represent something much more fundamental about how we relate to each other. This thing, that is fundamental regardless of culture, is based on the idea that we must both **give and receive** in order to make a relationship function properly. Let's examine this idea in further detail.

Giving and Receiving

The Mohawk native North American tribe has a proverb that translates, "Life is both giving and receiving". In human interaction, we often say that we need to give and take. Sometimes we give and receive visible things from each other such as food, money, gifts etc., but sometimes we cannot physically "see" what we are giving and receiving. For instance, if I say I will do our laundry if you clean our dishes, most of us would interpret this as giving and receiving. What is it that we are giving and receiving (or taking)?

There may be no particular word in English that is used for what we are giving or taking but some other languages use words that seem highly related to this "thing" we are giving and receiving. For example, some people say that the word "chi" in Chinese, the word "ki" in Japanese, or the word "prana" in Indian refers to this "thing" we are giving and receiving. In many ways it is something we seem to gain when we receive attention and something that we seem to lose when we are forced to pay attention to someone. When we receive attention from others, we feel energized and happy. When we are forced to pay attention to someone, we feel de-energized and often uncomfortable. Thus, perhaps the closest word to this thing we are giving and taking in the English language may be **energy**.

When we are paying attention to others, we are **giving energy**. More specifically, we are attending to the needs or desires of other people when we give energy. When others are attending to our needs or desires we are **receiving**

energy. When we demand others to attend to our needs and desires, we are **taking energy**. We can all relate to this experientially. It feels depleting when we ignore our own needs and desires in order to attend to the needs or desires of someone else. In contrast, it usually feels energizing when other people go out of their way to attend to our needs and desires.

In our interactions with other people in our everyday lives, we take turns giving and receiving energy from each other. I do something for you and then you do something for me. I pay you money and you send me a product you are selling. I speak about my concerns and then you speak about your concerns. Most of our interactions as humans are structured in this way. Most of our interactions with the people around us are based on what Schank and Abelson (1977) call **scripts**. Scripts are cognitive representations of the order of behaviors in specific situations in life. Scripts determine what is socially acceptable and what is not in a particular situation. For example, if I receive excellent service in a restaurant, I leave (give) a generous tip. I do not shine the shoes of my waiter or waitress. Scripts help us understand conventional ways to give and take in human interaction. Although giving and taking (or giving and receiving) is universal to humans, the specific ways we give and take may be culture specific. In any culture, we have guidelines about how to give and take in various common situations (e.g., in a restaurant) and this helps everyone in the interaction process maintain their energy levels. No one feels too depleted and no one feels too energized. People who do not follow the scripts of society are often considered to be maladjusted in society. In fact, theorists such as **Erving Goffman**, (1974) and **Thomas Szasz** (1961) believe that people who are diagnosed with **psychological disorders** are merely people who **do not follow the conventional scripts** of society.

Within the conventional scripts of society, we develop our own unique interpersonal patterns as individuals. Some of these unique interpersonal patterns are conducive to healthy relationships and others are detrimental to relationships. Since people with the detrimental interpersonal patterns are the one's who need the most help, many clinical psychologists focus on these negative types of interpersonal patterns (e.g., Luborsky, 1984; Strupp & Binder, 1984). These unique interpersonal patterns are assumed to develop from the unique personal experiences of each particular individual through **trial and error** and **modeling**. For example, if I only receive attention (i.e., energy) from my parents when I cry, I will repeat this behavior every time I feel I need attention (i.e., energy). Or, if I see my father intimidating others (i.e., taking energy) to get what he wants, I may try that on my peers in the playground. If it works, I may repeat that over and over in my life. Furthermore, many of these patterns are designed to occur in a

never-ending cycle (Leary, 1955, 1957). For example, by behaving in a dominating way toward my little brother I pull a submissive response from him. As a consequence, my brother responds submissively and this response pulls a dominating response from me again. My dominating response again, pulls a submissive response from my brother and this cycle can go on and on. This would be an example of myself having a repetitive pattern of taking energy from my little brother.

As we can see from these examples, many of our problematic interpersonal behavior patterns involve ways to take energy from other people. Because of our selfish nature, we sometimes take much more energy than we give. James Redfield (1993), the famous spiritual writer, often refers to this as **stealing energy**. Just as everyone is selfish to some extent, everyone steals energy to some extent. Throughout our lives, we have all developed different ways to steal energy from others because it makes us feel energized and feeling energized feels good. There are more patterns of stealing energy than there are people, but the most common interpersonal patterns of stealing energy can be divided roughly into a number of categories. I have outlined below some of the most common general patterns of stealing energy.

High maintenance / high expectations
—being overly demanding of others
—expecting others to be the way we want them to be regardless of how that person feels

Interrogation / criticism
—making others seem inadequate by being critical of them (by interrogating or criticizing)
—makes the self feel better than others

Intimidation / anger
—making others fear the self with intimidation and/or expressing anger

Self-pity / guilt trip
—making others feel sorry for the self or feel guilty for not being compassionate

Buttering up (the Boss)
—making people do things that we do not want to do by telling them that we are not good at it and they are better at it

Aloofness / charisma
—making others interested in the self by holding out information

Chainchatting
—speaking incessantly without listening to others
—demanding attention incessantly without letting others have their turn

Yes, I know but…
—asking for suggestions and advice
—responding to the suggestion or advice by expressing that the suggestion or advice is not what we are looking for
—purpose is not to solve the problem but to receive attention

Passive Aggression
—doing things primarily to cause an emotional reaction (e.g., concern, annoyance, anger) in someone else
—subtle types of behaviors to receive attention from others

One-upmanship
—making the other person feel inadequate by stating that we are better than the other person in some way

Avoidance
—avoiding others who we feel are likely to steal our energy
—not a method of stealing energy but rather a method to protect the energy that we have

We all steal energy and chances are, we have used many of these patterns listed above at some time in our lives. The difference between stealing energy and taking energy is only a matter of degree. Sometimes we steal energy and then the other person steals energy back from us, just as we can take energy and then give energy with someone. In fact when we are in the process of developing a relationship with someone, we are usually trying to figure out how the giving and taking will work in the relationship. We may first try our favorite ways of taking energy and if that doesn't work, we try something else. If we find some method that works, we like the person and try to develop that relationship. If we don't find that any of these methods work, we are not attracted to the person and often find someone else. At the same time, the other person is doing the same thing to us. These people are trying out their favorite methods of taking energy and we are sending them signals of whether we will allow them to take our energy in that way or not by responding to them in a variety of ways. For instance, if the other person tries the self-pity method and we ignore him or her, we are sending a message saying that we will not allow the other person to take energy from us that way. If, on the other hand, we listen to him or her whine and provide the person with pity, we have sent him or her a sign saying, "I will allow you to take energy from me in this way" and the person may be more inclined to use that same method on us again. If both people are able to find a method of taking energy from the other person that works, the relationship develops. If only one or neither person finds a method that works, the relationship disintegrates.

After two people have developed a relationship in this way, we begin relying on each other to take or receive energy from. This is one of the reasons why we become so attached to people we have close relationships with. Although we have been focusing on two person relationships, our actual lives involve more than two people. This applies to relationships with more than two people. For example, Jack may have a pattern of taking energy from Jill and Jill may have a pattern of taking energy from Jane and Jane may have a pattern of taking energy from Jack. Real life is usually much more complicated than this but I trust that you see the picture. In many ways, we could say that energy moves in cycles somewhat like currents in the ocean (see Figure 1). This implies that whenever we give or take energy, we are being influenced and are influencing the whole cycle of energy around us in some way.

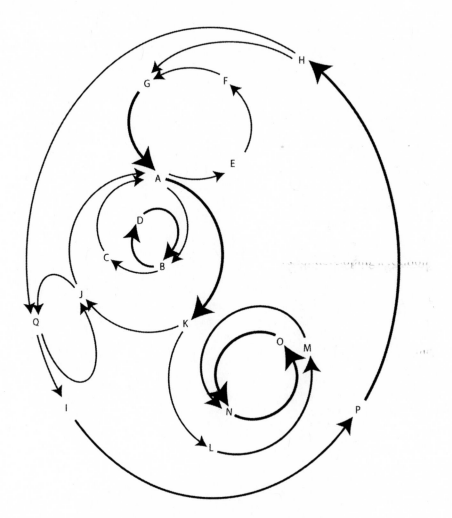

Figure 1. Energy Flow among Numerous Individuals

Internal Conflict Model

The Root of Unhappiness

You may have noticed in your everyday lives that some people are not bothered very much when someone else seems to be stealing energy from them. You may also have noticed that some people are bothered at the smallest things in someone else's behavior even though most people would not care about it. They feel that the other person is stealing their energy even though most people would consider the same behavior inoffensive and ordinary. Why does this happen? The reason why this happens is that giving and receiving energy is more a matter of perception than a matter of reality. Let's examine this by using what I call the **internal conflict model** (Sato, 2003).

The essence of the internal conflict model is simple. When things are going our way, we are comfortable. When things do not go the way we want it to, we feel discomfort. All of this has to do with **what we desire** (or need) and **what has, is, or could happen** (see Figure 2). When what we desire (or need) matches what has, is, or could happen, we feel comfortable. When what we desire (or need) does not match what has, is, or could happen, we feel anxiety or some sort of discomfort. If I feel upset that a bully took my lunch money last week, what I desire (to keep my lunch money) does not match what happened (the bully took my lunch money). Therefore I feel discomfort. On the other hand, if I was able to keep my lunch money, what I desire would match what happened and I would feel fine. If I feel uncomfortable because my friend is driving his car recklessly, what I desire (my friend to drive safely) does not match what is happening (my friend is driving recklessly). If I am worried about my next test, what I desire (to do well on the test) does not match what I think could happen (to do poorly on the test).

No Conflict - No Anxiety

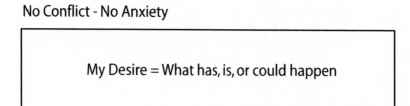

Conflict - Anxiety

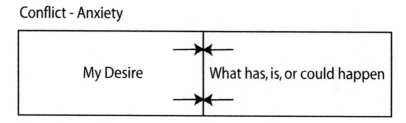

Figure 2. Internal Conflict Model

In order to manage our discomfort or anxiety, we usually try to do things so that what we desire wins over what has, is, or could happen. If what we desire does not match what has happened, we may repress or deny what happened in order to reduce our anxiety. If what we desire does not match what is happening, we may take control of the situation and change something about the situation so that our desires come true. If what we desire does not match what could happen, we may take control of the situation and do something so that our desires are more likely to come true. In other words, one way to deal with anxiety is to make our desires win over what has, is, or could happen.

The other way to manage anxiety is to do exactly the opposite. We can make what has, is, or could happen win over our desires. We can let go of our desires and just accept what has happened, what is happening, or what could happen without any resistance. Although this may be difficult to do in many circumstances, it may be more adaptive in some situations than trying to take control. We all know that being overly controlling can sometimes cause problems. Sometimes letting things (i.e., our desires) go is a much easier way to deal with our internal conflict than to take control. If I am upset that I had a car accident, letting go of my desire to avoid car accidents and accepting the event may be easier than trying to deny and repress my memory of having a car accident. If all of my friends want to go to the movies even though I want to go bowling, letting go of my desire to go bowling this time may be easier than trying to convince everyone to go bowling with me. In sum, there are two ways we can manage our internal conflicts. We can either make our desires win by taking control of the situation or we can let go of our desire and accept whatever has, is, or could happen. Figure 3 is an illustration of these two methods.

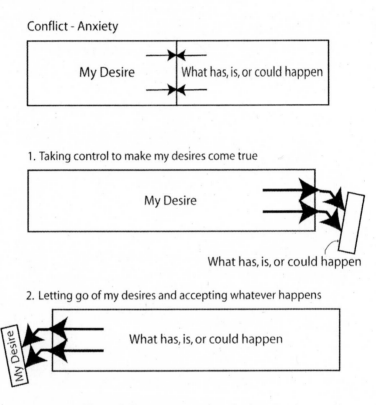

Figure 3. Two ways to reduce Anxiety

How does this relate to giving and taking in a relationship? What does the separation of my desires from what has, is, or could happen mean in the context of a relationship? When we have a relationship of giving and taking with someone, the relationship we are experiencing is not directly with that person. The relationship is in our mind. We are actually separating our desires from what has, is, or could happen and my self represents my desires and the other person represents what has, is, or could happen. The conflict is not really between my self and the other person but between my desires and what the other person did, does, or could do (i.e., what has, is, or could happen). If the other person does something that is not consistent with my desires, I feel like the other person is taking my energy. In this case, I feel like I have lost energy because my desires are losing the battle between "my desires" and "what has, is, or could happen" and I feel that the other person represents "what has, is, or could happen". And because the other person represents "what has, is, or could happen", I feel like the other person took my energy. If the other person does something that is consistent with my desires, I feel like I am receiving energy from the other person. This is because my desires are winning the battle between "my desires" and "what has, is, or could happen" and the other person represents what has, is, or could happen. Figure 4 is an illustration of how these factors relate to each other.

No Conflict - No Anxiety

My Desire = What has, is, or could happen

‖

My Self = Other People / Things (e.g., desires of others)

Conflict - Anxiety

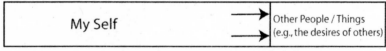

Giving and Receiving of Energy

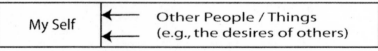

Self receives (or takes) energy from Other People / Things

My Self	← Other People / Things (e.g., the desires of others)

Other People / Things receive (or take) energy from Self

Figure 4. Correspondence between Internal and External Relationships

What this tells us is that our relationships with others are a reflection of the relationships between our desires and "what has, is, or could happen" in our minds. Whenever we experience a conflict with others, it is a reflection of conflict within ourselves. Thus the quality of our lives is really a reflection of our internal state of mind. Conflict of any kind is a sign that our desires do not match what has, is, or could happen and that we are holding onto our desires and resisting what has, is, or could happen.

Positive and Negative Emotions

Another important thing the internal conflict model tells us is that both **positive** and **negative arousal** are two sides of the same experience. When I feel anxious, it is because I am worried that what has, is, or could happen is winning over my desire. When I feel excited, it is because I feel like my desire is winning over what could happen. Either way, in order to feel any emotional arousal, we must be experiencing internal conflict. We must be in a state where our desire does not match what has, is, or could happen.

This is actually the key to the difference between people who are **optimistic** and people who are **pessimistic**. People who are pessimistic tend to compare what has, is, or could happen to something better that they desire. I wish I were slimmer than I actually am. I wish I had more money. I wish my spouse were a better person. When we do this, we automatically feel bad about our present situation since what we desire is always losing to what has happened or what is happening. People who are optimistic tend to think of their internal conflicts in a way that makes them feel like their desire is winning over what has, is, or could happen. Instead of thinking that they want to be slimmer, they think, "I am glad that I am in good health." Instead of thinking that they want more money, they are thankful for what they have. These people compare their present state to negative things that could have happened to them. When we do this, we automatically desire our present state over what could have happened and this makes us feel like our desire is winning over what has, is, or could happen.

An interesting study reported by Medvec, Madey, and Gilovich (1995) illustrates this difference quite effectively. They compared the emotional experiences of silver medallists and bronze medallists in the Olympics and found that the bronze medallists reported more positive emotion than the silver medallists. Since most silver medallists compared their silver medal to receiving the gold medal, they feel unhappy. They see the situation as their desire losing to what happened. On the other hand, since bronze medallists typically compare receiving the bronze medal to receiving no medal at all, they feel very happy that they received a medal. These people tend to see the situation as their desire winning over what could have happened.

The main point here is that people who are optimistic and happy about life have the intuitive ability to manipulate their thoughts in a positive way (Seligman, 1991). Regardless of what happens, they can think of their experiences so that they feel like their desire is winning over what has, is, or could happen. Because of this, they are always able to find something to be happy about. They are always able to find something positive in everyone and everything. They are always able to find something to be grateful about. Although some people may be naturally born with these abilities, these abilities can be learned and developed. We can all learn to become more optimistic and happier if we know how to and are willing to make the effort.

The root of all unhappiness is internal conflict. We are only unhappy when what we desire does not match what has, is, or could happen. This is really the essence of the theory developed by the humanistic psychologist Carl Rogers (1959). **Carl Rogers** states that anxiety, discomfort, or unhappiness occurs when our self-concept does not match our experiences. He calls this a state of **incongruence** since the two do not match. The **self-concept** in his theory corresponds to my desires and **experience** corresponds to what has, is, or could happen. When these two things do not match, we feel anxiety. When these things do match, we feel no anxiety. We feel comfortable. Rogers calls this state **congruence** since the two things match with each other.

The more incongruence we experience, the more anxious we are. This is the state of having many unresolved issues (or internal conflicts). As mentioned in the previous paragraphs, the more we resolve these issues by either taking control or letting go of our desires, the more we can be at peace with ourselves. Since many of our issues concern our negative experiences in our past, letting go of our desires is often a more mature way to resolve our issues than taking control and making our desires come true. For example, if I am unhappy because I lost a tennis match, letting go of my desire to win that match may be easier than going back in time and winning that match.

According to Rogers (1961), the more unresolved issues we have, the more anxious (or unhappier) we are. Rogers states that the process of resolving our issues one by one is our road to happiness. It is the process of moving from a state of incongruence to a state of congruence. He calls this the process of **becoming fully functioning**. This process, according to Rogers, is a never-ending process since we are never completely free of internal conflict. It is impossible to have a life where everything goes the way we want it to. And since there are things that do not go the way we want it to, we inevitably experience internal conflict (or incongruence) over and over in our lives. Therefore, we need to keep resolving our internal conflicts (or issues) throughout our lives.

The Process of Letting Go

The internal conflict model also allows us to explain why **forgiveness** sets ourselves and not only other people free. When we cannot forgive someone, we are refusing to let go of our desires. We are refusing to let go of what we wanted the other person to do or not do. Therefore, we are experiencing internal conflict when we cannot forgive someone. If we let go of our desire (i.e., what we wanted the other person to do or not do), we can naturally accept what the other person did or did not do. In other words, letting go of our desires allows us to forgive. This is why many people say that we must forgive more for ourselves than for the other person. When we forgive, we set ourselves free from our own internal conflict.

Whether it is forgiving someone or accepting anything that does not match our desires, this feat is much easier said than done. How can we accept things that do not match our desires? I am afraid I have no easy answer for that question. In many cases, it is a slow, difficult, and emotional process. Some researchers suggest that the **five stages of death and dying** by **Elizabeth Kübler-Ross** (1969, 1975) apply to any painful experience that requires letting go of our desires (Wortman & Silver, 1989). Kübler-Ross suggests that when we are faced with death we experience five emotional stages. The first stage is **denial**. This usually occurs when we are first informed that we will die soon. In the beginning, we are in shock and are unable to accept this fact. The second stage is **anger**. This is where we blame others for our death as well as envy others who are able to live longer than us. The third stage is **bargaining**. During this stage, we try to negotiate with others who might have some control over our fate such as doctors as well as angels and divine beings in order to prolong our lives. This is usually unsuccessful and we end up in the stage of **depression** after this. At the earlier parts of this stage we lose hope and begin feeling like there is nothing we can do to avoid our destiny. This causes a type of depression that Kübler-Ross calls **reactive depression**. In the later parts of this stage, we experience a type of depression characterized as **preparatory depression**. During this time, our depression is focused primarily on the fact that we will not be able to enjoy the company of our loved ones after we die. We often cry during this stage to help us let go of our desire to live longer and accept our fate. Lastly, we complete the process of letting go of our desire to live longer and enter the **acceptance** stage. In this stage, we are calm and peaceful and learn to appreciate the remaining moments we have in this world.

As we can see, accepting death requires letting go of one of our strongest desires that we all have as human beings: the desire to live. Some researchers suggest that the five stages of death and dying discussed by Elizabeth Kübler-Ross apply to any painful experience that requires letting go of our desires. Although we may not experience all of the stages, there is often a similar emotional process when we let go of any desire (Saunders, 1989; Wortman & Silver, 1989). Although not everyone goes through all of those stages and some people may go through the stages in a slightly different order, most psychologists agree that the process of letting go of our desires is emotional in nature and ultimately ends with the acceptance of whatever we were resisting (what has, is, or could happen). This process of letting go of our desires and accepting what has, is, or could happen usually requires a significant amount of time. It takes time to let go. It takes time (sometimes hours & sometimes many years) for this emotional process to occur. In most cases, the more important the desire, the more emotional the process, and the more time we require to let it go. The people of the Hopi native tribe in North America have a proverb that translates, "Don't be afraid to cry. It will free your mind of sorrowful thoughts." As you may have noticed from your personal experiences, the emotional process of **crying** often allows us to let go of our desires and resolve our internal conflicts. This process of crying is often regarded as a part of the depression stage in Kübler-Ross' theory.

From the discussions above, it is clear that the more we let go of our desires, the more conflict free and anxiety free we could be. However, letting go of all of our desires seems to be an almost impossible task. For example, the desire to live or the desire to breathe or the desire to eat may be very difficult to give up. Perhaps it is impossible as long as we are living. Although I do not know since I have never experienced a state of no desires before, many individuals have discussed this state in the past. It is commonly referred to as a state of **complete transcendence**. In Buddhism, it is referred to as a state of satori. In Hinduism, it is referred to as nirvana. It is a state of mind where we are completely at peace with everything. We have no internal conflicts, no desires, and no anxiety whatsoever. We can openly accept anything and everything that happens without any resistance and are living completely in the present moment. There is no giving or taking of energy since we do not differentiate our desires from the desires of others. Some people try to experience a state of mind as close to this as possible by meditating, praying, chanting, fasting, as well as using breathing exercises and psychotropic drugs. Although I have not, perhaps some meditating monks in the mountains have actually experienced this complete state of transcendence.

For most of us mere mortals, however, many of our fundamental desires are inevitable. Furthermore, the desires of other people are real (we cannot let go of other people's desires). And therefore thinking about how to deal with our own desires and the desires of others is a very real question for most of us. Perhaps the best thing we can do given our lowly mortal circumstances is to attend to the desires of others and hope that others will attend to of our own desires. Since being respectful of others often leads others to be respectful of us, this may be a useful motto to keep in mind.

Early Development

Attachment

Before we exist on earth, we have no needs or desires as individuals. At birth (or perhaps conception) we begin having needs or desires. I tend to use the word "desires" more instead of needs because things we need are based on our basic desires such as our "desire to live" but they are essentially the same thing. From our experiences in life we know that not all of our desires are satisfied. From what we learned from the internal conflict model, we know that unsatisfied desires lead to internal conflict. This implies that the more desires we have, the more potential there is for unsatisfied desires. Moreover, the more unsatisfied desires we have, the more internal conflict we experience. As we grow older, we develop more and more desires and this can potentially lead to more and more internal conflict. The more our basic needs (or desires) in infancy and childhood are left unsatisfied, the more internal conflict we experience. Because caretakers are not perfect, some of the basic needs (or desires) of infants and young children are inevitably ignored or at least left unsatisfied. The more our needs are left unsatisfied, the more internal conflict we experience. This internal conflict manifests itself as insecurity in infants and children and many times these insecurities are carried over into adulthood.

One of the basic needs (or desires) of infants is physical contact. Parents often cuddle and stroke their infants to sooth and comfort them. As we grow older, these strokes are replaced with attention and respect, a symbolic representation of the physical strokes that we used to receive. The psychiatrist, **Eric Berne** (1964) refers to this as **psychological strokes**. Therefore, if we use Berne's terminology, we could say that a lack of psychological strokes leads to insecurities within ourselves.

One researcher who has contributed immensely on this subject is **Mary Ainsworth** (1979). The work of Ainsworth and her colleagues known as **attachment theory** suggests that the way a caretaker interacts with an infant influences the infant's emotional development (e.g., Ainsworth, Blehar, Waters, & Wall, 1978; Main & Solomon, 1986; Main & Weston, 1981). This line of research suggests that infant attachment styles can be divided into four categories and each of these categories is associated with distinct interactive styles of the caretaker. The first attachment style is known as the **secure attachment style**. The infant with a secure attachment style is emotionally stable and is adequately but not overly responsive to the environment. They are even tempered and adapt to new situations relatively quickly. This attachment style is very common among infants with caretakers who are very responsive and attentive.

The second attachment style is known as **insecure anxious ambivalent attachment style** or **insecure anxious resistant attachment style**. These infants are very emotionally unstable and frequently demand attention without being attentive to others (i.e., steal energy). This attachment style is very common among infants with caretakers who respond mostly to negative behaviors as well as caretakers who are inconsistent in their responses to their infants. Overall, this attachment style is common among caretakers who steal moderate amounts of energy from their infants. The third attachment style is known as **insecure anxious avoidant attachment style**. Infants with this style of attachment tend to be unresponsive and avoidant of not only their caretakers, but also to strangers. This attachment style is very common among infants with caretakers who are either unresponsive or overly controlling of them. As we can all imagine, if we are with a powerful (caretakers are more powerful than infants) but unresponsive or overly controlling person for a long time, we would become unresponsive and avoidant ourselves as a way to deal with that person. In general, this attachment style is common among caretakers who are either avoidant or steal excessive amounts of energy from their infants. The fourth attachment style is known as **disorganized / disoriented attachment style**. Infants with this kind of attachment style tend to be unresponsive and unpredictable in general. This attachment style is very common among infants with caretakers who are abusive to them. It is common among caretakers who steal extraordinary amounts of energy from their infants. It is considered to be the most insecure form of attachment.

These findings suggest that the more attentive, responsive, and caring the caretaker, the more secure the infant tends to be. **Margaret Mahler** (1968) suggests that in order to help infants develop secure attachment styles caretakers must interact in an attentive and caring manner with the infant. She describes this type of interaction extensively in her work and calls this **interactional synchrony**. When caretakers are interacting with infants in this way, both the caretaker and the infant feel an intimate sense of oneness with each other. It is a state of symbiosis in which each individual is responding naturally and smoothly to the other with perfect timing. The less symbiotic the interaction is, the more insecure infants tend to become.

Many psychologists discuss the importance of early life experiences in the formation of our personality. The reason behind this has much to do with social power. Having social power allows us to attend to the desires of others less. Conversely, having less social power forces us to attend more to other people's desires. In short, social power allows us to take more energy than give. Many times our basic needs (or desires) are not satisfied when we are very young since the primary people we interact with in this part of life are all more powerful than us (e.g., parents, older siblings, nannies, babysitters, teachers etc.). This allows caretakers and other people more powerful than the child to take more energy than give. Although caretakers and other people in power seldom do this intentionally, the relative powerlessness of children can be taken advantage of and children are often left feeling deprived of energy. Unfortunately, caretakers often take energy and sometimes steal energy from children to compensate for their own insecurities. By doing this, however, caretakers create insecurities in their own children without awareness. Object relations theorists discuss how infants and young children blame themselves instead of their caretakers when the caretaker steals their energy (e.g., Fairbairn, 1974; Guntrip, 1964). Because we as infants do not want to believe that our caretakers are selfish and unloving, we rationalize our caretaker's negative behaviors by convincing ourselves that they are stealing our energy because we are bad children, not worthy of attention and respect. This type of thinking is at the root of our insecurities. Thus when our basic needs are not met and others steal lots of energy from us and leave us depleted, we develop insecurities that lead to a sense of inferiority, low self-esteem as well as various psychological disorders in extreme cases. Although people steal our energy in adulthood and we do develop insecurities in adulthood as well, the deepest insecurities typically develop early in life because of our relative powerlessness during this time of life.

This is one of the reasons why **Carl Rogers** (1961) emphasizes that we need to be raised in an environment of **unconditional positive regard**. An environment of unconditional positive regard is an environment where we feel that we are loved, accepted, and respected just for being ourselves regardless of who we are and what we do. When we do not feel loved, accepted, and respected, we develop insecurities that lead to anxiety, low self-esteem, and depression. Although Rogers focuses more on adulthood personality rather than infant development like Ainsworth and Mahler, it is clear that his message is consistent with the developmental theorists.

Parenting Style

All of these theories focus on being loving and accepting of one's child (i.e., giving energy) but none of them discusses discipline and punishment (i.e., taking energy) in childrearing. Many of us have heard of the proverb, "Spare the rod and spoil the child". Don't we need discipline as well as love and care? The work of many developmental theorists suggests that these two things are actually more compatible with each other even though we tend to think of them as opposing things. The key is communication. When we communicate, we express ourselves but we also listen. Good communication involves both the giving and taking of energy. When a caretaker takes, he or she should also give. When a child gives, they should also receive. This is the essence of a positive caretaker-child relationship.

Diana Baumrind (1971) organized research findings in this area by discussing four different parenting styles and how each style influences the emotional development of the child. The first parenting style is labeled **authoritative parenting**. Caretakers with an authoritative parenting style respect the child's thoughts and feelings but also express their own desires and needs in a respectful manner. These caretakers are warm and nurturant but also provide guidance for their child. This makes the child feel secure and emotionally stable knowing that the caretakers truly care about him or her. Caretakers with an authoritative parenting style also serve as positive role models by valuing both the processes of giving and receiving, the key to continuous open communication. The second parenting style is called **authoritarian parenting**. Authoritarian caretakers are overly controlling, demanding, dominating, and restrictive towards their child. These caretakers have little regard for the child's thoughts and feelings and take much more energy than they give. These behaviors of the caretaker make the child become desperate to protect and replenish his or her energy. In order to protect his or her own energy, the child typically becomes avoidant of the caretakers. Moreover, in order to replenish the energy lost to the caretakers, the child typically develops patterns of stealing energy from other people such as peers and siblings.

The third parenting style is known as **permissive or indulgent parenting**. These caretakers suppress their own desires and needs to the point where the child is allowed to do almost anything he or she wants at any time. In this situation, the caretaker is accepting of anything the child does but provides very little guidance. In other words, the caretaker gives energy but does not take much energy. As is evident from this description, there is a lack of meaningful communication between permissive or indulgent caretakers and their children. This leads to both feelings of alienation and poor communication skills in these children. Because of these two factors, these children typically steal energy from others in order to avoid feelings of alienation. If this is unsuccessful, these children may give up on communication altogether and become avoidant. The fourth parenting style is known as **neglectful or uninvolved parenting**. As the name suggests, caretakers with this type of parenting style consistently neglect many of the important needs and desires of the child. The children of these types of caretakers receive very little care and attention and typically end up feeling neglected and unworthy of love and respect. In an attempt to receive the care and attention they need, these children typically steal energy from other people such as peers and siblings. If this is unsuccessful, these children may give up on communication altogether and become avoidant.

The general message is clear. Good communication with both sides giving and taking equally is the key to optimal emotional development. If caretakers take much more than give, the children develop insecurities. If caretakers give much more than take, the child feels alienated and loses out on the opportunity to develop the social skills necessary to build secure relationships. The reason why many theorists emphasize that caretakers should give rather than take has much to do with the power difference between caretaker and child. Because caretakers are more powerful than their children, they can and often do to take more than they give. We as caretakers do not need to remind ourselves to take energy because it is a natural human tendency to do so anyways. However, it is often useful to remind ourselves as caretakers that we need to give because we are human and have the strong tendency to become selfish and greedy, even with our children. Although both giving and taking are important, it is more common to make the mistake of taking too much than giving too much.

From what we have learned until now, the two most common ways that we develop insecurities are: (a) insufficient care of our basic needs and, (b) experiences of having energy stolen from us. The more our basic needs are left unsatisfied, the more insecure we become. The more others steal energy from us, the more insecure we become. Because of the ways insecurities typically develop, they are intricately related to a sense of powerlessness and inferiority. **Alfred Adler** (1954) discusses how our **inferiorities** form the basis of our personality. He suggests that the motivation behind most of our behaviors and thoughts are to compensate for our inferiorities. We are motivated to make personal achievements to compensate for our inferiorities. We form groups in order to compensate for our inferiorities. We steal energy from others to compensate for our inferiorities. All of these things allow us to compensate for our inferiorities by making us feel more powerful. In sum, inferiorities make us do many things that our insecurities make us do. Both make us feel conflicted inside and both contribute to our experience of anxiety.

Dealing with Anxiety

Regardless of whether we think it is inferiority, insecurity, or internal conflict that causes it, the experience of anxiety has been examined by a variety of theorists. **Anna Freud** (1946) discusses how we all use **mechanisms of defense** (denial, repression, rationalization, reaction formation, projection etc.) in order to **reduce our anxiety levels. Carl Rogers** (1959) discusses the **process of defense** (e.g., denial, distortion) as a way to reduce our anxiety levels. Although these defense mechanisms/processes are unavoidable and useful in reducing our anxiety levels, we pay a price for it. They require energy and leave us with less energy that can be used for other purposes. Because defenses leave us with internal conflict at the subconscious level, they reduce our ability to handle stress in other aspects of life (Baumeister, Muraven, & Tice, 2000; Freud, 1966). Therefore, defense mechanisms/processes are best used as temporary fixes that should be dealt with more thoroughly later (when we are emotionally strong enough and prepared) since they are never the real solution to a problem.

Another way to reduce anxiety is to **steal energy** from others. We often steal energy from people less powerful than us because they are the ones that will allow us to steal energy from. It may be our family members, friends, schoolmates, coworkers, neighbors, or even complete strangers. Just as a drowning person will grab at anything to keep him or herself from drowning, we take energy from anyone we can take it from when we are highly anxious. Unfortunately, our own children end up being the most common victims of our habit of stealing energy. This occurs much less out of ill intent but more out of convenience (although this does not make it acceptable). Our children are always around us and we have more social power than they do. When we are anxious, we respond instinctively by stealing energy from our children without being aware that we are actually doing it. Unfortunately, this typically creates a negative cycle of passing on our insecurities from one generation to another since we create insecure children when we steal energy from them, and they will steal energy from their own children later on in life in order compensate for their own insecurities and inferiorities (i.e., to reduce their anxiety).

We also steal energy from individuals other than our children such as siblings, roommates and romantic partners (and parents when we become older). When we steal energy from others who have approximately equal amounts of social power, the others typically steal energy back. If I do something nasty to my roommate, he or she becomes more likely to do something nasty to me. When others steal energy back from us, we are motivated to steal energy back from them again. Therefore, we usually end up being caught in our own negative cycle of stealing energy back and forth when we respond to our anxieties by stealing energy. Insecurities and the anxiety that it causes are at the root of all interpersonal conflict. The more insecure we are, the less stable our relationships tend to be. Insecurity is caused by internal conflict and therefore the more insecure we are the more we see things as "me vs. someone else" rather than "we" functioning together as one single unit.

Another thing we can do in response to anxiety is to **avoid** others. When we are anxious and the people around us are more socially powerful than us, we cannot steal energy from them. Chances are, they will steal energy from us if we interact with them. When we are insecure and anxious in these situations, we become avoidant. Although we cannot replenish our energy this way, at least we can prevent others from taking our energy. This is how some of us become avoidant of other people. When we avoid in response to our insecurities, we end up feeling alienated and lonely and being alienated and lonely makes us even more insecure and anxious. Being more insecure and anxious often makes us even more avoidant of others and again, we end up being trapped in our own game.

Research in **attachment theory** supports the notion that our insecurities make us either steal energy or become avoidant. Researchers such as Hazan and Shaver (1987) followed up on Ainsworth's original work on infant attachment and found that our attachment styles formed early in life influence our behavioral patterns in adulthood (especially with romantic partners). According to work in this area, individuals with secure attachments are able to form stable trusting relationships with close others in adulthood. Individuals with anxious ambivalent/anxious resistant forms of attachment, however, tend to be very possessive and suspicious of close others in adulthood. Because of these characteristics, these individuals tend to steal energy from others close to them in an attempt to make them stay close and loyal to them (even though this strategy often backfires). Furthermore, individuals with anxious avoidant attachment styles tend to stay avoidant of others even in their close relationships in adulthood. Whenever they feel anxious, they tend to avoid the problem they are facing. Because their experiences tell them that interacting with close others when faced with a problem often drains their energy, anxious avoidant individuals avoid interacting with close others to protect their own energy. As we can imagine, this makes it difficult for these individuals to develop and maintain close meaningful relationships with others. Finally, individuals with disorganized/disoriented attachment styles have difficulty forming close and meaningful relationships with others because of their unpredictable behavior patterns. Their behavior patterns consist of engaging with others by stealing energy or disengaging by being avoidant.

Anxiety caused by our insecurities is also an excellent motivator for personal achievement. Personal achievements allow us to gain "respect" from others. It also allows us to assume positions of social power in many cases. The more **social power** we have, the less other people can steal energy from us and the more we can steal energy from them. Therefore, the more insecure we are, the more we crave for social power. Indeed many of us who are in positions of social power (like myself) are merely insecure individuals underneath our facade of composure and elegance.

Insecurity and anxiety also motivates us to **form and join groups**. Being a part of a group relieves us of anxiety because it makes us feel like we are not the only ones who feel insecure about a particular thing. We often form groups with individuals who have similar insecurities. Having similar insecurities cause us to have similar desires from the perspective of the internal conflict model. This is why we all have the tendency to form groups with people who have the same desires as us. We form groups with people who have similar political agendas. We form groups with people who like similar things such as music, celebrities, physical activities, cultural activities, and sports teams. This allows us to validate our own insecurities and also increases our chances of making our desires win over what has, is, or could happen. For example, my insecurities may drive me to support a certain political party. If I join a group of people who also support this party (i.e., people who have the same desire), I feel more secure. If I recruit more people to join this group and have more people vote for this party, I increase my chances of my desire winning over what could happen (e.g., my political party winning the elections). Thus the more insecure and anxious we are, the more motivated we are to form and maintain our own groups.

All of the reactions to anxiety discussed above involve hoarding energy. We are either trying to protect what we have left or trying to obtain more. From what we learned about internal conflicts, we know that there is another way to deal with anxiety. Instead of taking control and making our desires win over what has, is, or could happen (e.g., taking energy from others), we can deal with our anxiety by **letting go of our desires**. As discussed earlier, letting go of our desire enables us to accept what has, is, or could happen without resistance and resolve our internal conflict. When we mature in life, we overcome our insecurities and we overcome our insecurities by learning to let go of our desires. The more we are able to do this, the more we **develop socially, morally, and emotionally**. The more we develop in this way, the more we see things as "us" rather than "me vs. you" or "us vs. them". The more we are able to do this, the deeper the unity we feel with a wider variety of people and things around us and the more mature we become as human beings.

Visual Analogy of our Experiences

The Ocean Analogy

In order to develop a better understanding of our experiences, I have devised something called the ocean analogy (Sato, 2003). Let's think of ourselves as hollow entities with numerous tubes as walls around it (see Figure 5). The numerous tubes form a shell around us to protect us from the dangers of the outside world just like our skin protects us from the outside world in some ways. The tubes around us are filled with air so that we can float on the ocean water. Let us also assume that there is some space between the tubes so that water and air can pass through us quite freely. Figure 5 provides us with a two-dimensional diagram of this image and the tubes are represented as doughnut shapes around a hollow opening representing each individual. There is nothing but air or water in our bodies and we can increase or decrease the thickness of the walls on the outside of the tubes but cannot increase or decrease the amount of air inside the tubes. The thicker we make the walls on the outside of the tubes, the smaller the space between the tubes. Making our walls thicker has numerous effects. It makes air and water inside and outside of the person flow through less freely. It also makes the person heavier and makes the person sink deeper into the water.

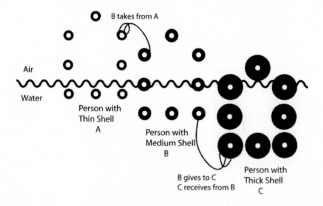

Figure 5. The Ocean Analogy

In contrast, the thinner we make the walls on the outside of the tubes, the larger the space between the tubes. This makes air and water inside and outside of the person flow through more freely. This also makes the person lighter and makes the person rise to the surface of the water. Each entity represented by tubes and the hollow space inside represents one person. The air represents energy and the water represents anxiety or the absence of energy. We will refer to the openings between the tubes as **pores** and the material on the outside wall of the tubes as **shells**. When we are defensive, we make our shells thick and our pores small. Conversely, when we are relaxed and easygoing, we make our shells thin and our pores large. Furthermore, just as we can never cease to interact with the environment, we can never completely close our pores.

According to this ocean analogy, the point of the game is to feel that we have as much air (i.e., energy) and as little water as possible. Because we can never completely close our pores, this means that we must stay afloat. The more air we have in our body, the more energy we feel, the more water we have, the more depleted of energy we feel. A person can open or close his or her pores as much or as little as he or she wants. The more we thicken our shells and close up our pores, the more we constrain the air and water from traveling in and out of our body. This makes it difficult for water to come inside and deplete us of energy (at least temporarily) but it also makes us sink deeper into the water because we become heavier (due to the thick heavy shells). Sinking deeper into the water eventually allows water to seep in and makes us feel depleted of energy (remember that we can never completely close our pores). In contrast, the more we open our pores, the easier it is for the water to flow in and out of our body and the higher we float. As mentioned before, the air represents energy so we tend to feel energized when we have lots of air inside of us. Furthermore, when we have lots of air (or energy) inside of us, we are able to relax and open up our pores because we are not afraid of running out of air (i.e., filling up with water). The less air we have inside us, the more afraid we become of running out of air and our natural tendency in response to this is to close up our pores to avoid losing even more air.

When we take energy from others, it is like grabbing onto the other person, pushing them down and using them to stay afloat. Naturally, nobody wants to be pushed down into the water because we lose air this way. When we are pushed down into the water, we have two natural reactions. The first is to grab onto someone (usually the person that just pushed us down because he or she is conveniently in our presence at this moment) to prevent our selves from sinking. The other reaction is to thicken our shells to protect water from coming in. As you can imagine, none of these reactions are very constructive in the long run. The first reaction usually traps us in a negative cycle of taking turns pushing each other down into the ocean. The second reaction makes us eventually sink into the ocean and lose air. These two reactions correspond to the two common responses to anxiety (i.e., stealing energy and avoidance) discussed earlier.

We can take energy by pushing others down to stay afloat. We can give energy by pushing other people up or allowing others to push us down. We can also receive energy by others pushing us up. When we give and receive energy, we are taking turns essentially pushing each other up (or down) and trying to stay afloat in the ocean (see Figure 6). Here's the dilemma of social life. If we close up our pores, we are more likely to protect whatever air (i.e., energy) we have inside us since the air within is more constrained to stay inside us and others are less likely to push us further down since they know that we will not be of much help (we are not floating very high). Others may even avoid us for fear that we will push them down to float higher. At the same time, however, we also sink deeper into the ocean and eventually the water seeps inside and we lose air (depleting us of energy). On the other hand, the more open our pores are, the more useful we are for others who are sinking to grab onto because we can help them stay afloat the most. This makes us targets for people with thick shells (because they are sinking). If we think of this in another way, however, this also makes us more giving and helpful to others. Moreover, the thinner our shells are, the more we are able to stay afloat without any help from others.

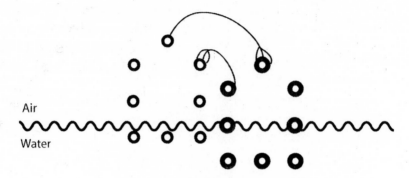

Two Individuals taking energy from each other

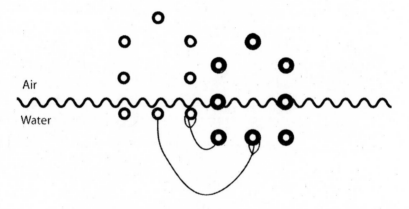

Two Individuals giving energy to each other or
Two Individuals receiving energy from each other

Figure 6. Giving, Receiving, and Taking Energy

To sum up, we tend to close our pores under two types of circumstances; when others push us down (i.e., take our energy) and when water begins seeping in from the bottom (although neither of them make sense in the long run). We tend to open our pores under two types of circumstances as well; when we have lots of air inside and when we feel unafraid of anyone or anything pushing us down. When our pores are open and have lots of air in us, we usually feel comfortable and relaxed. When we are filled with water, we feel anxious, defensive, self-protective, sometimes even angry and aggressive, and sometimes sad and depressed. This is when we have our problems. This is when we feel unhappy.

You may have guessed by now but the shells represent our internal conflicts and the insecurities that they cause. The more internally conflicted and insecure we are, the thicker our shells tend to be. This implies that our own internal conflicts and insecurities make us lose energy. The more insecure we are, the more we lose energy. We lose energy even if no one is taking energy from us.

Although there are slight individual differences, we are all born with thin shells. The more our basic needs are left unsatisfied, the more we believe that life is difficult and the world is a tough place and that we need to protect ourselves from it (i.e., the more defensive we become). Therefore the more our basic needs are left unsatisfied, the thicker our shells become. Moreover, the more other people push us down, the thicker our shells become to resist water from coming inside. In contrast, the more our basic needs are satisfied and the less people push us down, the thinner our shells remain. The thinner our shells remain, the more we float and the more energized we feel.

This is nice for people who have never developed thick shells but what about the rest of us who have thick shells now? What do we do if we have developed thick shells? What we must do is to make our shells thinner again by unlearning things from our experiences. If I experience having much of my energy stolen from me repeatedly, I become afraid that others are going to steal energy from me again in the future. This makes me scared, defensive, avoidant and sometimes even angry and aggressive. This is the state of having a thick shell. In order to make my shells thinner, I need to unlearn the things I have learned from my experiences. In order to unlearn I must let go of my desires, which enable me to let go of my defensiveness, insecurities, and inferiorities. My main desire is to protect my energy and I must let go of that to make my shells thinner. This allows me to open up my pores again and float higher and become more energized and less anxious. I must stop worrying about what others will do to me. If others steal my energy, that's fine. If they don't, that's fine too. As long as I keep my shells thin and pores open, I always float back up and become energized even if someone temporarily pushes me down. As you can imagine, this is easier said than done. This process is the same as the process of letting go of our desires in the context of the internal conflict model discussed earlier. It is often a long and difficult process but one that is almost always worthwhile in the long run. Once our shells become thinner, we are able to stay more energized and emotionally stable, become more easygoing with others, and are able to live our lives more naturally and gracefully with minimal levels of stress.

Self-Group Identity

One of the things we have learned until now is that thick shells make us anxious and alienated. However, like any rule, there are exceptions. Even if we have thick shells, we can be open and easygoing with certain people that we feel comfortable with. We discussed earlier about how insecurity and anxiety motivates us to **form and join groups**. Being a part of a group relieves us of anxiety because it makes us feel like we are not the only ones who feel insecure about a particular thing. We often form groups with individuals who have similar insecurities. Matching insecurities means matching desires. We learned earlier that we like people who have similar desires. As **Fritz Heider** (1958) discusses in his work on **Balance Theory**, if two people like (or desire) the same thing, it is highly probable that they will like each other. Conversely, if two people like each other but they do not like (or desire) the same thing, there is a high probability that one or both of them will change their mind so that they both end up liking the same thing. In other cases, two people may not like each other initially but end up liking each other because they have found a common desire. You have probably seen many movies where two people who initially do not like each other end up liking each other after they face a common enemy. This is a classic example of how groups form. Two people who initially do not have matching desires end up having matching desires because of this common enemy. Both want to win against this enemy. When we form a group with others, we essentially open our pores toward others but not toward the rest of the world. The shells are thick toward everyone else but the people we like (i.e., have matching desires with). Figure 7 is an illustration of this state using the ocean analogy. When we are in this state of mind, we think of "us" instead of "you vs. me". If we both do things that are consistent with both of our desires, we both feel energized. This is the experience of interpersonal or group unity. This is why we feel unity with people who have the same desires as we do. When I do something to satisfy my desire, the other person feels like his or her desires are being satisfied as well. We feel like we are sharing our energy. My air is your air. Whatever happens to you feels like something happening to me. When we are in this state, we attend to, respect, and care for each other more than we care for others outside of our group.

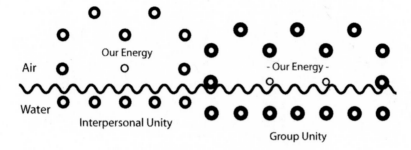

Figure 7. Interpersonal and Group Unity

In this case, we both feel energized not because we are receiving energy from each other but because we change our perception of what our energy is. We now perceive our energy as the air inside both of us instead of only the air inside ourselves as individuals. Because there is more air inside both of us together than any one of us individually, we feel energized when we unite with groups. Although I explain much of this as if there are only two people involved, this can occur among multiple individuals and not only between two individuals.

In sum, this is how it works. When two individuals have opposing desires, they tend to become enemies and try to steal energy from each other. When two individuals have matching desires, they experience a sense of unity with one another. When two individuals have non-matching but compatible desires, they may not experience a sense of unity with each other as much but have the opportunity to develop a balanced relationship by giving and receiving equally. When a large number of people have matching desires, they are all able to experience unity with each other.

Group unity is the source of group identity and scholars who study **Social Identity Theory** often discuss how there are **various levels of group identity** (Hogg, 1992; Turner, 1987). Some of these groups are much larger and include others whereas some partially overlap with other groups to varying degrees (see Figure 8). For example, we may identify ourselves as members of our nuclear family but also identify ourselves as members in our religious group and at the same time, identify ourselves as members of a certain gender as well as members of our country. Some of these groups may be more important to us than other groups but as a general rule, the more we feel like we are sharing energy with a certain group, the more important the group is to us.

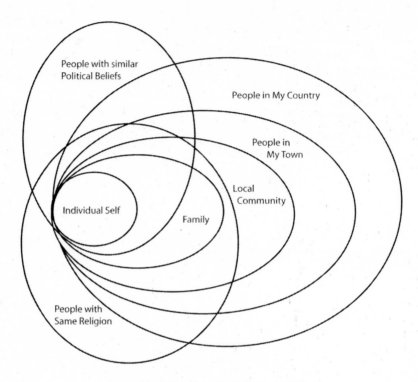

Figure 8. Various Levels of Group Identity

Classic research by **Henri Tajfel** (1981) on the **Minimal Group Paradigm** has shown us that group identification (matching desires) is a natural human tendency. Even the remotest differences such as seating location between people make us categorize ourselves as one group and as distinct from others. Moreover, the more important the group is to us, the more biased we become against other groups. This occurs because whenever we form a boundary to define ourselves as individuals or as a group, we automatically create a category of others that are outside of that boundary. This automatically makes us respect and attend to the needs and desires of the people inside our boundary more than the people outside of it. **Marilynn Brewer** (1991, 2001) elaborates on this idea in a unique way. Her work on **Optimal Distinctiveness Theory** suggests that we all have the tendency to identify with certain groups but also have a need to feel that our groups are unique and different from others. We want to be the same as some people (matching desires) but also feel uniquely different from some others.

Both of these motivations serve unique purposes. We are motivated to belong to certain groups so that we feel like we have more energy than we do as individuals. Our need to feel that our group is uniquely different from others comes from our need to feel that we are better than certain others. Therefore, we want our groups to be uniquely better than others because that enables us to justify taking energy from others. It enables us to think, "We are better than you so you should pay attention and learn from us." Although it is not pretty, this is the natural reaction all humans have when we feel insecure. When we are insecure, we not only find others who are similarly insecure and form groups but we also create outgroup members to steal energy from to compensate for our own insecurities.

Although feeling that we belong to a group allows us to feel more secure and stable, it can also be the root of group conflict characterized by narrow mindedness, prejudice, and mob mentality. From the perspective of the ocean analogy, interpersonal conflict can be characterized as two people pushing each other down to float higher. Similarly, we have group conflict when two groups are trying to float higher by pushing each other down and using each other as floatation devices (see Figure 9).

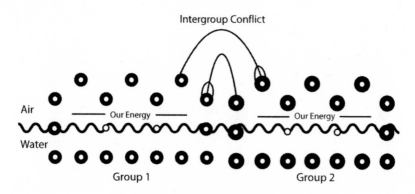

Figure 9. Intergroup Conflict

Transcendence in the Ocean

From the previous sections, we learned that there are two ways to replenish our energy from an interpersonal perspective. The first is to take or receive energy from others and the other is to form groups and share energy with others (Sato, 1998, 2001, 2003). Not surprisingly, various interpersonal theorists have conceptualized interpersonal behaviors on two dimensions corresponding to these two methods (Leary, 1955; McAdams, 1985; Sullivan, 1953). The dimension corresponding to taking or receiving energy is often labeled dominance, power, or control. The dimension corresponding to sharing energy is often labeled affiliation, warmth, intimacy, or love. Just as there are various levels of taking and sharing energy, these theorists claim that interpersonal behaviors can be understood by examining where they lie on these two dimensions[1].

If we step out of the interpersonal perspective and step into an intrapersonal perspective, we realize that there is yet another way to replenish our energy. Earlier, we discussed how complete transcendence is a state of mind with no desires and therefore no conflict. If we use the ocean analogy to describe the state of **complete transcendence**, it is when our shells are so thin that they disappear. It is a state with infinitely open pores (see Figure 10). It is a state without any boundaries. If I am completely transcendent, I do not differentiate myself from other people or other things. Everything is one (i.e., in unity). In fact, philosophers like **Alan Watts** (1966) often discuss how **boundaries are merely artificial lines drawn in our minds**. They discuss how all matter (or energy since matter is made of energy) is connected. The air around me is always connected to me. The air around you is always connected to you. The air around me and the air around you are connected with each other. Therefore you and I are actually connected. In fact, everything is connected. Everything is one[2]. Boundaries are not real lines out there in the physical world. We create them only out of convenience. It is convenient and useful to think of the chair that I am sitting in as separate from me because it allows me to assume that the chair does not come with me when I stand up and go to the bathroom. The point is, however, that the chair and I are not physically separate. They are only perceived as separate in our minds. A state of transcendence is a state in which we feel this deep spiritual unity with all of these things and do not distinguish ourselves from anyone or anything else in the world. When we are in this state, we feel highly energized because we identify with all of the air around us and not just the air inside of us (as an individual) or inside of our group (because we have no concept of "I" our "my group" as separate from anything or anyone else). No one can take energy from us and there is no need to take energy from others. Because we do not differentiate ourselves from others, taking or giving energy is not only meaningless but is inconceivable.

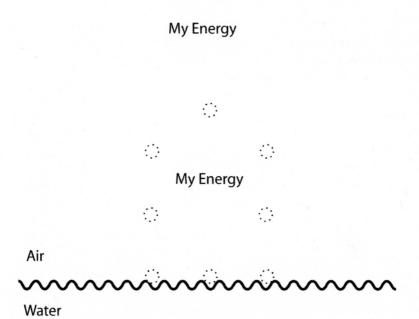

Figure 10. Complete Transcendence

You may have noticed the inherent contradiction in this explanation of complete transcendence. If complete transcendence is a state of no boundaries, why are we distinguishing between a state of transcendence and non-transcendence. This distinction should dissolve if we experience complete transcendence and we should not be concerned about experiencing transcendence. In fact, the earlier description of complete transcendence is not actually completely complete transcendence. It is something close to total transcendence, but there is one more step in order to experience completely complete transcendence. Complete transcendence occurs when we identify with and are in harmony with everything and everyone. **Completely complete transcendence** occurs when we go beyond that. We realize that there is no "I". Therefore, there is nothing to identify with and nothing to be in harmony with and nothing to interact with. We are not our bodies, we are not our minds, we are not the cosmos. The "I" does not exist. Completely complete transcendence is just accepting whatever is being experienced and letting everything and everyone be the way they are. When we realize this, it doesn't matter if we have a relationship, it doesn't matter if we are in harmony or not, and it doesn't matter if we have reached transcendence. Nothing matters. There is no good and there is no bad. Everything just "is".

Some people may say that this is dangerous because this may allow people to steal and kill and do terrible things because nothing matters anymore. In fact, even if people did those seemingly terrible things, it wouldn't matter to us if we were experiencing completely complete transcendence. If we were experiencing this state, it would not matter to us if someone was killed or if someone was robbed. It wouldn't even matter if we were robbed or killed because we don't distinguish life from death and we don't distinguish our property from other people's property. Moreover, if we are experiencing completely complete transcendence, we would not be motivated to kill or steal because it does not matter to us if someone is dead or alive, and it does not matter to us if we take something or if we don't. It should make no difference to us if we are experiencing completely complete transcendence and thus the idea of doing anything like that (or doing anything for that matter) would never cross our mind.

The Self-system

Defining the Self-system

Let us change gears a little bit and examine these experiences from the perspective of the self-system. The **self-system** is an understanding in our minds that enables us to maintain the energy necessary for us to both psychologically and physically survive. The self-system contains an elaborate program saying, "The world works like this and I can do this and this to maintain my energy." We know from our personal experiences in life that every situation requires a unique response. The self-system consists of our repertoire of things we can do to maintain our energy in a wide variety of situations. For example, we can take control of the situation in a variety of ways (i.e., take energy) or reconceptualize the problem so that we feel like our desires are winning. Or, we can let go of our desires and accept what is happening. Depending on the exact nature of the situation, we choose to respond in different ways and our self-system helps us to make the best choice possible by providing a variety of possible responses and its consequences from our memory of similar situations in the past. The more intelligent we become, the more we are able to take control (i.e., take energy) or reconceptualize the problem so that we feel like our desires are winning. In contrast, the more we mature as human beings, the more we are able to let go of our desires and accept what is happening. The development of the self-system refers to the development of all of these different strategies to deal with these situations. In sum, the wider the variety of experiences we have, the more our self-system develops. The more developed our self-system, the more we are able to maintain a consistent level of energy in a wider range of situations effectively. This is why many people say that direct personal experience is more valuable than anything we can learn from books or classroom lectures.

Development of the Self-system

Although every response we make is guided by our self-system, every experience including the response and its consequence modifies the self-system as well.

Because no two experiences are exactly the same, every experience in life is something new. And because every experience is something new, our self-system is never equipped with a complete understanding of the present experience. Every experience requires us to modify our understanding of the world and how we maintain our energy in it. Thus in order to respond appropriately to each of our experiences, our self-system needs to be broken down, modified, and rebuilt again into something that enables us to understand and respond to all of the situations we have encountered before as well as the one we just encountered. This implies that learning and growth is a constant process of rebuilding our self-system. More specifically, as **Jean Piaget** (1973) noted, learning and growth involves two processes. One of these processes is known as **assimilation**. Some experiences are very similar to a previous experience we had. When this happens, we require minimal change in our self-system. We only need to widen the applicability of the understanding that we already had. This is known as assimilation. With assimilation, we register the new experience somewhere in our already existing self-system. The other process is called **accommodation**. If a new experience is very different from any previous experience, we break down and reconfigure the self-system so that it incorporates an understanding of the new experience in addition to all previous experiences. Since no experience is neither exactly the same as a previous experience nor incomparably different from any previous experience, every new experience requires a combination of both assimilation and accommodation. Some require more assimilation than accommodation and others require more accommodation than assimilation.

When an experience requires more accommodation than assimilation, we usually do one of two things. One of the things we could do is **repress or deny the experience**. If our self-system finds this experience too threatening to our self-system, we often deny or repress the experience and try to continue our lives as if we did not experience that event. Sometimes our experiences are extremely shocking or too traumatic for us and we find ourselves unprepared to digest this experience. Sometimes, we are merely too fearful and lazy to adjust our self-system. In either case, we refuse to allow the event to influence us and try to stay in our own comfortable shell. Although this may help us feel safe, it prevents our self-system from developing.

The other thing we could do in the face of a new event is to **accept the new experience** and break down our self-system temporarily until it reconfigures itself so that all of the experiences already in our self-system plus the new event become part of the new self-system. By doing this, we allow the self-system to truly grow and develop. Therefore, every step of development is one **cycle of chaos and sta-**

bility. When we truly allow a new experience to influence us, we temporarily experience chaos when our self-system breaks down. When our self-system rebuilds itself again, everything is understandable again and we return to a stable state of mind. In the same way, every step of development is also a **mini-experience of transcendence**. Each time the self-system takes a step in its development, it develops into something that transcends but includes the previous self-system (because it makes sense of the all of our previous experiences plus the new experience we just had). Therefore, as mentioned before, every step in development makes us more comfortable with a wider range of situations and experiences.

Interpersonal Applications

Since the self-system consists of a memory of all experiences and how to respond to them, it can be applied to interpersonal experiences. If we apply this to interpersonal experiences, the self-system is our understanding of how we deal with a variety of people in a variety of situations so that our energy level is maintained. Furthermore, taking energy from others can be considered as the act of influencing and causing others to modify their self-systems. In contrast, giving energy to others can be considered as the act of allowing others to influence and modify our self-system. Every time we interact with others (i.e., give and receive), we modify our self-system because every time we give, we are influenced and this makes us modify and adjust our self-system. On the other hand, every time we interact, we are also influencing and causing the other person to modify his or her self-system. Thus, **interaction** is a constant process of **influencing** and **being influenced**.

The self-system can also be considered as a **comfort zone**. It consists of what we are familiar with from our past experiences. The more our experiences are similar to what we have experienced before, the more we are able to stay within our self-system. The more we are functioning within our self-system, the more we can just repeat what has worked in the past to maintain our energy level. In contrast, the more we experience something different from anything we have experienced in the past, the more we are taken outside of our self-system. The more this happens, the more we must adjust and modify our self-system. However, the more we do this, the more inclusive our self-system becomes (i.e., the more we develop). Because encountering the same things saves us from modifying our self-system, we tend to like things that are familiar. This is why we like familiar things, familiar people, and familiar places (Bornstein & D'Agostino, 1992). Research on interpersonal attraction, for example, reveals that we tend to like people we are familiar with and that we also tend to like people who are similar to us (Bornstein, 1989; Byrne, 1971). This is the reason why. We tend to like people who are similar to us because we know what to expect. It is also why we tend to repeat the same behavioral patterns over and over again. In many cases, although stepping out of our comfort zone is usually conducive to our development, we are sometimes too fearful and lazy to step out since modifying and adjusting causes temporary internal chaos and requires much energy.

It takes work to rebuild a new self-system and the process is often painful. If the process seems overly painful, we'd rather ignore the new experience and stick with what we already have. This is the experience of **resistance**. It is like having a **thick shell around our self-system**. Our self-system consists of various scenarios of dealing with a variety of situations. It consists of strategies concerning when to make our shells thin and let go of our desires, when to make our shells thick, and when to take energy from others and who to take energy from. However, the self-system itself also has a shell around it (see Figure 11). When we thicken the shells around our self-system, we are resisting change. When we make our shells around the self-system thin, we are being open, accepting of new experiences, and constantly modifying and adapting our self-system. In fact, our repertoire of things we can do to maintain our energy in our self-system provides us with a good indication of how thick the shells around our self-system are. The more our repertoire consists of making our shells thick and taking energy from others (i.e., being defensive and aggressive), the thicker the shells outside of our self-system are (i.e., the more resistant we are to change). The more our repertoire consists of making our shells thin and letting go of our desires, the thinner the shells outside of our self-system are (i.e., the more open and accepting we are of change and adjustment). Figures 12 and 13 illustrate the relationships between our repertoire of responses in our self-system and the thickness of our shells on the outside of our self-system. Therefore, regardless of whether we are referring to the shells inside or outside of our self-system, the thinner our shells, the more we are influenced but the more efficiently we adjust and develop and learn from our experiences. Furthermore, the thinner our shells are, the more we are able to let go of our desires and remain in unity with other people/things in a wider variety of situations[3].

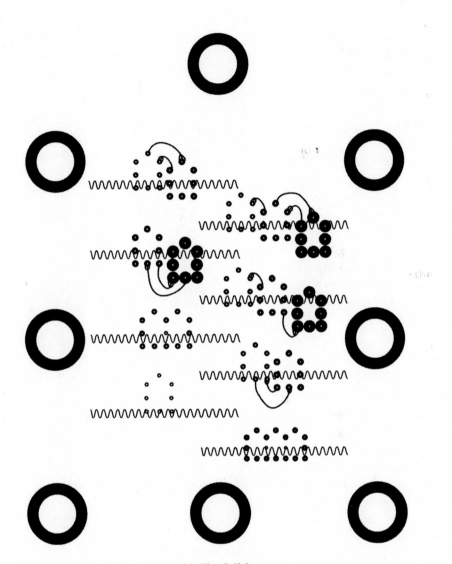

Figure 11. The Self-System

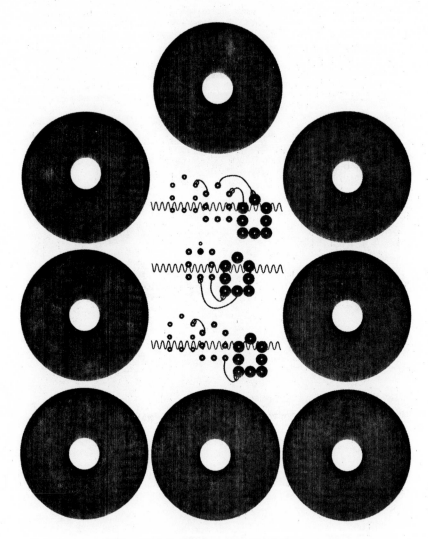

Figure 12. Self-System with Thick Shells

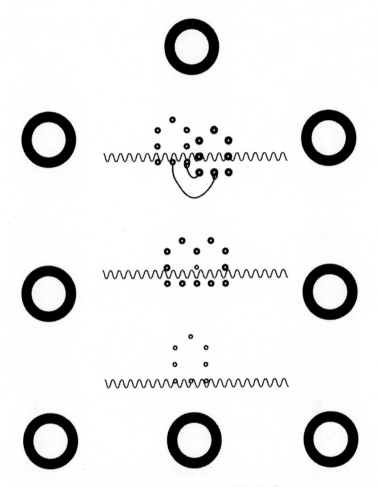

Figure 13. Self-System with Thin Shells

Intrapersonal Applications

Let's apply what we have learned about the self-system to our internal experiences. **Self-esteem** is an internal experience that is commonly discussed in our modern culture today. If we apply this concept to the ideas about the self-system discussed earlier, we realize that self-esteem is a reflection of how large our comfort zone is. It is a reflection of how much our self-system can accommodate. If we have a self-system that enables us to deal well with a wide variety of different situations, we are able to maintain our energy level in a wide variety of situations. This enables us to stay in our comfort zone more and thus makes us feel happier with ourselves in general. This is the state of high self-esteem. In contrast, if our self-system is not well developed, we feel like we are outside of the comfort of our self-system more frequently. This makes us feel defensive, become avoidant and sometimes even behave aggressively. This is the state of low self-esteem. We frequently feel high levels of anxiety because our self-system is not developed enough to deal with many of the situations we encounter in our lives. We are constantly alert and cannot relax because we do not have a set pattern to deal with many of the situations we encounter. Therefore, the more we are able to remain in the comfort zone of the self-system regardless of the variety of situations we encounter, the more self-esteem we have. This is why our self-esteem grows when our self-system develops into more sophisticated systems as we gain more experience.

Self-confidence is very similar to self-esteem although **self-confidence** is often conceptualized as situation specific rather than a global personality characteristic (like self-esteem). We have self-confidence in situations where we are able to stay within the comfort of our self-system. That is, we are self-confident when we already have set patterns in the way we deal with a situation. We know what to pay attention to and what to ignore, and we have a set pattern on how to respond to the particular things that happen in the situation. When we are in a situation that we are not familiar with, we are jolted out of the comfort of our self-system and we lose some confidence because we have no set patterns in the way we respond to the situation. As a result, we typically try to protect our own energy and take energy from the environment (i.e., become defensive and aggressive). In sum, the more we function outside of our self-system, the more anxious and defensive we feel and the more we tend to behave awkwardly and sometimes even aggressively. In contrast, the more we are functioning within our self-system, the more confident and calm we feel and the more composed we behave. It seems that if we are completely functioning within our self-system, however, we become bored. It makes us feel like we are stagnating in our personal growth. However, if we are forced too far out of our self-system we become anxious and defensive. There is a delicate balance needed so that we neither feel bored nor anxious and defensive. Let us examine how this balance works.

In order to examine this, we need to go back to the internal conflict model discussed earlier. According to the internal conflict model, there are two ways to deal with internal conflict. One was to take control and make our desires win over what has, is, or could happen and the other was to let go of our desire and accept what has, is, or could happen. Although it has not been discussed before, there is a third way to deal with internal conflict. The third way is the middle road. It is to stop perceiving the situation as, "my desires versus what has, is, or could happen" and making our desires equal to what has, is, or could happen. To do this, we need to simultaneously accept and act upon what is happening. Although this seems like we are doing two incompatible and contradictory things at the same time, people do this all of the time. This is what is happening when athletes and artists talk about being in "**The Zone**". When we are successful at doing this, it feels like we are paying attention and accepting what is happening but at the same time we feel like we are in control because we are actively participating in the process (of what is happening). This is often described as a mysterious and sometimes even spiritual experience because it is so difficult to describe in words.

In a regular situation when we are not in "The Zone", it feels as if we are accepting what is happening at one moment and then, considering the situation and taking action to make our desires come true in the next moment. After that, we accept what is happening in the next moment as a result of our actions and then we take control and do something again to make our desires come true in response to what is happening at this point. This is not only what occurs when we give and receive energy interacting with other people, but it is a standard process of interacting with anything in our environment. When we are in "The Zone", this process occurs so fast that the boundary between accepting what is happening and taking action becomes undetectable. One follows the other so quickly that it is experienced as a smooth continuous process. It is just like when we see a computer screen and see smooth continuous lines and shapes rather than thousands of separate tiny pixels. Because we experience "The Zone" as continuous, it feels like we are accepting what is happening at the same time as taking action to make our desires come true. In other words, we experience no boundary between my desires and what is happening. It makes us feel like our desires equal what is happening (see Figure 14). In interpersonal experiences, this is the experience of people interacting on the same wavelength. It is when two people feel like they are "clicking" with each other. In this type of interaction, it feels like we are simultaneously giving and receiving energy with each other and none of us is losing any energy. Because no one is losing energy, it is commonly considered to be a mysterious and special experience of interpersonal unity.

Conflict - Anxiety

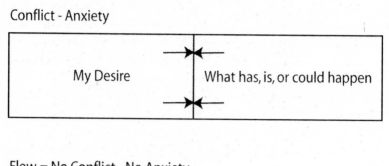

Flow = No Conflict - No Anxiety

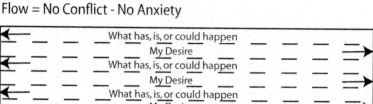

Flow = No Conflict - No Anxiety

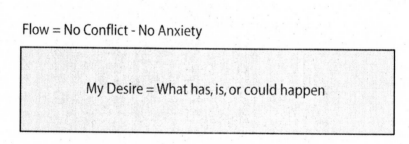

Figure 14. How "Flow" resolves Internal Conflict

Mihalyi Czikszentmihalyi (1991) discusses this balanced state by using his concept of the "**Flow**". Czikszentmihalyi claims that there is a specific state of mind that he refers to as "Flow" that causes optimal performance on tasks as well as a sense of happiness. Flow is defined as being completely absorbed in the process of an activity rather than the end goal. In order to experience "Flow", the activity must be perceived as challenging but not too difficult. When the activity is perceived to be too easy, we become bored. When we perceive it to be too difficult, we feel anxious and frustrated. In order to experience "Flow", we need to be pushed just outside of our self-system but not too far outside of our self-system. In order to feel happy, we need to feel that life is somewhat challenging but not too challenging.

By conducting research on this phenomenon, Czikszentmihalyi noted some of the most common characteristics of "Flow". The first of these characteristics is that our **attention is completely absorbed** by the activity. When we are experiencing "Flow", we are completely focused on the present activity and nothing else enters our mind. The second important characteristic is that in order to experience "Flow", the activity we are engaging in must be **perceived to have a goal or direction**. Although the goal is not the focus, we need to have some idea about what we are trying to accomplish with this activity if we want to experience "Flow". The third characteristic is that we must be **open to clear and immediate feedback**. The essence of "Flow" is to be engaged in the activity and the only way to stay completely engaged in any activity is to constantly pay attention to what is going on every moment of the way. The fourth characteristic of "Flow" is that we **experience a sense of control** when we are in this state of mind. Because we are actively participating in the process, we feel like we have control over what is happening. The fifth characteristic of this state is that we **lose self-consciousness**. Because we are completely absorbed in the activity, we no longer experience the self as separate from what we are interacting with. The sixth characteristic is that we **lose a sense of time**. When we are completely absorbed in an activity, time seems to go by much faster than usual. In some rare cases of "Flow", Czikszentmihalyi has noted that time seems to go by slower than usual.

The "Flow" can be experienced with any type of activity, not only sports and art. It can be experienced when we are mowing the lawn, washing our dishes, speaking to a family member, or filing documents in our office. Czikszentmihalyi notes that people who are happy have the ability to organize their experiences so that they spend more time experiencing "Flow" in their lives. He suggests that we can all consciously try to experience more "Flow" by changing how we perceive our experiences so that they are seen as challenging but not too overwhelming. When something is boring, we can change our perception of the activity to make it interesting. For example, sweeping the floor may be a boring activity at first, but if we focus on forming particular shapes with the dust we are sweeping, it may become an interesting activity. When something seems overwhelming, we may try to break it down into smaller manageable steps so that it feels less overwhelming. Writing a twenty-page report for our job may feel too difficult and overwhelming at first. However, if we break it down by writing one page in the morning and one page in the afternoon every day for ten days, it may feel less difficult and perhaps even interesting. This is the essence of mindful living. In order to feel happy, we need to pay attention to each moment and participate in each step of the process rather than focusing on the end goal. This allows our self-system to naturally develop without feeling overwhelmed.

When we are not able to experience "Flow", we are resisting something. Although we discussed resistance as a thick shell around our self-system, let's examine this concept further using the internal conflict model. If we use the internal conflict model to understand **resistance**, we could say that resistance is **refusing to accept what has, is, or could happen**. Or, we could say that resistance is refusing to let go of our desires. Resistance is a state of **internal conflict**. It is a state of defensiveness and often a **source of interpersonal conflict**. In an interpersonal context, what has, is, or could happen is often what the other person desires. Refusing to accept what the other person desires is a common cause for interpersonal conflict. It makes the other person feel disrespected and sometimes even rejected. Resistance is also a **source of intergroup conflict**. If one group refuses to accept the desires of another group, the other group feels disrespected. This is the most common cause of intergroup conflict. Therefore, regardless of whether it is interpersonal or intergroup, we need to be open to each other. In order to make a relationship flourish, we must allow others to influence us and break down our self-system and keep rebuilding it again and again. This is the essence of good communication. Communication is a continuous process of breaking down and rebuilding our self-system. People change. People's circumstances change. People's desires change. In order to keep any relationship working, we need to be constantly open to those changes and adjust accordingly each moment we interact. This is why staying open and respectful to others as well as continuous communication is so important in relationships.

When we are faced with an experience that requires us to make considerable adjustments in our self-system, we often try to resist. However, in many cases we eventually make this adjustment after an emotional process of letting go of our desires. Although we discussed the emotional process of letting go of our desires using the theory of Elizabeth Kübler-Ross (1967, 1975), the work on intercultural communication by **Stella Ting-Toomey** (1998) may also provide us with some important insights concerning this process from a slightly different perspective. According to Ting-Toomey, there are **four stages** in developing communication skills when we move to a new culture. The first stage is known as **unconscious incompetence**. It implies fundamental ignorance of the scripts, expectations, and interaction patterns of the new culture. The person in this stage may interpret other people's behaviors incorrectly and respond awkwardly without being consciously aware of being "out of sync" with everyone else. The second stage is known as **conscious incompetence**. In this stage the person is consciously aware that the people in the new culture have different expectations and scripts but do not completely understand what they are. People in this stage are soaking up information but often experience awkward pauses and silences due to misunderstandings. The third stage is called **conscious competence** or the 'mindful' stage. In this stage, we cognitively understand the communication patterns of the new culture and are making a conscious effort to interpret others and respond to them in a new way. However, because we are not used to it at this point, our behaviors do not flow naturally with the people in the new culture yet. The fourth and last stage, known as **unconscious competence**, is the stage where we begin to think and respond naturally in the way the people in the new culture do. Communication becomes spontaneous and smooth. It is like learning to drive a car or ride a bicycle. First we must make a conscious effort to move our hands and feet in a certain way. After a certain amount of practice, however, it becomes spontaneous and natural. We no longer need to "think" about what we are doing. Ting-Toomey states that we become "mindlessly mindful" in this final stage.

We can see that the work of Ting-Toomey applies to not only developing communication skills in a new culture, but all situations requiring an adjustment of the self-system. As mentioned earlier, it can be applied to situations in which we learn physical skills such as driving a car or riding a bicycle. It applies to any situation requiring any change in a person, whether it is to stop smoking, start exercising, or becoming a better listener. It can also be applied to situations in which we adjust to having new people in our lives such as a roommate, a spouse, a child, or in laws. In all of these situations, we are forced to modify our self-system. At first, we may not realize there is a problem but at some point we notice. Noticing makes us self-conscious and this makes us become awkward and clumsy because we do not know what to expect and how to respond to the new situation. As time goes by, however, we learn. We start making a conscious effort to change and as more time goes by, we become so used to the new situation that our behaviors become natural and spontaneous.

Practical Implications

Abuse of Social Power

As discussed earlier, having social power allows us to take more energy than give. Given this assumption, it is clear that individuals in positions of social power should refrain from abusing their power as much as possible. Most of us are in a position of social power in at least some of our relationships. We may be an older sibling, a manager, a scout leader, a coach, a parent, or just a child who is physically bigger than another. As people in social power, we need to be careful not to abuse the power that we have. If we do abuse our power and consistently take energy from people who have less power than us, we make those less powerful more insecure. The more we do this, the more insecure they become, and the more they will steal energy from other people who are typically less powerful than them. This is why parenting is often considered to be a crucial factor in personality development (even though there are many other factors).

As parents and other caretakers of children, we should not abuse our social power because we create insecurities this way. By stealing energy, we create people who live a life of insecurity and steal energy from others. This does not mean that parents should become pushovers and not tell children what to do or what not to do. As suggested by the work on parenting discussed earlier, it means that parents (or any other person in power) should respect, listen and pay attention to their children (or anyone less powerful) and attend to their needs as well as guide and direct their behaviors in a respectful manner. As parents, we should demand respect but we should also respect the desires of our children just as much. As managers, we should respect the desires of our workers just as much as they respect us. Even though people who are in positions of social power are often tempted to abuse their power for their own benefit, it is extremely important to resist that temptation.

Resisting our own temptations to abuse our power and trying to stop stealing energy is easier said than done. Nobody has had a perfect life. We all have internal conflicts and we all have insecurities. Because we have these insecurities, we all have developed patterns of stealing energy. Even though some do more than others, everybody steals energy and everybody abuses their power to a certain extent. Yes, that includes you and me. We may not be consciously aware of the fact that we do this, but we all do.

The main point is this. We have a choice to contribute to this world either in a positive or negative way. We are all participants in this world and whatever we do influences everything that goes on in this world in some way. So if we take more energy than we give from many people around us, we are contributing to making this world full of people who are desperate to replenish their energy. In contrast, if we live harmoniously and respectfully with everyone in the world, we are increasing the number of people who are respectful of each other and are able to live in harmony with each other. It is clear that there are people who take our energy even when we are respectful and attentive to them, and we may not feel the positive effects of our behaviors in any immediate way. However, by doing this we are making a small but extremely important contribution to the evolution of the world. We are increasing the chances of this world to move towards more peace, unity, and harmony. This is because the more we care, attend to, and respect others, the less energy others lose and the less insecure others will be and the less they will be motivated to steal energy from others.

Four stages in Close Relationships

Let's look at another practical application of the theories we have been discussing until now. Recent work on interpersonal relationships suggests that there are four general stages in the development of an interpersonal relationship (Sato, 2003). These stages apply to a variety of relationships such as close friendships, roommates, romantic relationships, work relationships, and even parent-child relationships to some extent. It may also be important to note that even though they will be explained primarily in the context of a two-person relationship, this applies to relationships among more individuals as well (although the more people involved, the more complex it becomes).

1. Mutual interest stage

The first stage characterizes the very beginning of a relationship. For a relationship to develop, both individuals must be interested in forming a relationship with the other. In order to form a relationship with each other, both individuals must be interested, accepting, and respectful of the other to a certain extent. Each person must attend to the other's desires to a certain extent. In other words, each must provide the other with some energy. Nobody wants to form a relationship with a person who does not attend to our desires at all. When both individuals are interested in forming a relationship because they receive energy from each other to some extent, we have a beginning of a relationship. This is how most relationships begin. We do not know each other well in the beginning and so we are very interested in each other in this stage. We pay attention to each other and we are respectful of each other. Everything about the other person seems new and interesting. In addition, we often feel energized during this stage because one of our primary desires match. We both desire to maintain the relationship.

This applies to all types of relationships including romantic relationships. It refers to the "Falling in Love" phase in the beginning of a romantic relationship. Although, the emotional impact of this stage is much more pronounced in romantic relationships because various additional hormones and social expectations are involved, the underlying dynamics are still the same.

2. Power struggle stage

After a while, both individuals get to know each other very well and begin paying less attention to each other. Even though we are now committed to the relationship to a certain extent, the novelty wears off (and the spark in the relationship is gone) and the other person is not as interesting as before. We begin paying less and less attention to each other, and we begin respecting each other less and less. The honeymoon is over. We stop appreciating the other person's existence and we start getting annoyed at the little things they do. We begin taking each other for granted and begin trying to use the other person for our own personal benefit. We begin wanting to change the other person into what we want him or her to be like regardless of what the other person wants. This happens with romantic couples, roommates, friends, co-workers and anyone that we have known for a while. In other words, we begin trying to take more energy than we give to the other person.

When we are in this stage, we often find ourselves having arguments and fights trying to decide who is more powerful or who is right. Do I attend to your desires or do you attend to my desires. Regardless of what we argue about, the underlying message is the same. "You attend to my desires!" "No, you attend to my desires!" Each individual wants to be the most powerful one in the relationship so that he or she can have his or her desires attended to most of the time. This is why we tend to fight and argue often in this stage. We are essentially fighting for social power.

During this stage, we often feel depleted of energy because the other person steals energy from us. When we feel depleted of energy, we have a natural reaction commonly referred to as the fight or flight response (Gottman, 1995). Although there are various names for this state, I will use the term "**emotional hijacking**" coined by **Daniel Goleman** (1995). Emotional hijacking is a natural neural and hormonal reaction that makes us extremely aroused, alert, and responsive when we feel we are in danger. This system has enabled our ancestors to survive through various types of dangerous situations. Although this mechanism has helped us survive, it sometimes impedes us from behaving constructively. The type of responses available to us when we are emotionally hijacked is either to fight back or to escape from the danger. When we are in this state, we become so emotionally involved in trying to protect our energy that nothing else matters. As a general rule with all organisms, the more aroused we become, the narrower our range of attention and shorter our attention span (Goleman, 1985). This implies that when we are emotionally hijacked, the less patient we are with others, the less we see the bigger picture, and the more we see things from our own self-centered perspective. We only think about why we are right, why we deserve attention and respect, and why the other person is wrong and is doing something unjust and unfair. We can't see things from the other person's perspective. We can't see things from a third person perspective either. When this happens to both individuals, both have no choice other than to fight for energy or leave. As you can imagine, neither of these responses seem constructive if we want to develop a relationship with someone.

Although this sounds tragic, there is also something positive going on in this stage. While we are fighting for power, we are also negotiating how, when, and how much energy we can take from each other. We are trying to see what works. We are both trying to find out how, when, and how much the other person allows us to take his or her energy. We are, in a sense, testing each other out. We want to know how much we can get away with. In this stage, we are trying out various interpersonal patterns to see what the other person will allow and when they will allow it. It is largely a process of trial and error. For example, I may find out that the other person does not allow me to steal energy from her by intimidating her but will allow me to steal lots of energy by interrogating and criticizing her in certain circumstances. At the same time, the other person may find out that I allow her to steal large amounts of energy from me by being aloof and charismatic but only allow her to take a tiny bit of energy from me by chainchatting or interrogation. In this way we figure out ways to take energy from each other and sub-consciously try to arrive at an agreement about how, when, and how much energy we allow each other to take from us. Once we arrive at an agreement, we settle into the relationship even more until at least one person in the relationship wants to change the agreement. If this happens, there is usually a negotiation period often accompanied with lots of arguments and fighting again until we arrive at a new agreement.

When two people keep interacting with each other even though they seem to dislike each other, they are typically in the power struggle stage. In this case, both still want to have a relationship with the other. Both individuals cannot leave the other alone because both want to show the other that he or she is the more powerful one and is therefore in control of the relationship. They are striving to come to an agreement about how, when, and how much energy each person will allow the other to take from them. When they come to an agreement on this, the power struggle is over. We notice from our experiences, that some power struggles are more dangerous and hurtful than others. The point is not to eliminate the power struggle (because that would mean eliminating the relationship) but to engage in the power struggle in as constructive a manner as possible. In many cases, the relationship may come to an end at this stage if the parties do not come to an agreement and lose motivation to maintain the relationship because they are tired of negotiating. In a marital relationship, this is typically when people file for divorce.

3. Codependence stage

As mentioned earlier, when we come to an agreement about how and how much energy can be taken from each other, we settle into the relationship even more. Even though we are not consciously aware of this in most of our relationships, each of us knows how much energy we can take from the other, and how (and in what circumstances) we are allowed to take energy from the other. At this stage of the relationship, the rules of the game are established and now the game is played over and over.

Even though we may not be completely satisfied with the relationship, if we reach this stage, we have settled for what we have. We become used to this type of interaction and we begin to expect it out of each other. And because it is expected, we feel uncomfortable if it does not happen. Therefore, we not only expect the other person to take our energy in a certain way but we begin to desire it. In a sense, there is a certain amount of unity between the two people in the codependence stage because both individuals are behaving according to what the other person desires. Although we do not have matching desires, we have compatible desires. Furthermore, we have now become dependent on each other to take energy from. We now need each other to compensate for our insecurities. This is why this stage is called **codependence** (Beattie, 1997; Mellody, 1989).

It is important to remember, however, that this is a simplified model of what really happens. There is no clear-cut line that divides the power struggle stage from the codependence stage. The cycle of giving and taking energy from each other does not repeat in exactly the same way all of the time. Even though both parties have settled on the basic rules, there is still a continuous negotiation of the rules at a microscopic level. The negotiation may not be as heated as in the power struggle stage, but things happen in life, circumstances change, and our patterns are constantly changing at a microscopic level.

4. Deep mutual respect stage

After spending considerable time in the codependence stage, some of our relationships gradually change in a positive way. Little by little, we begin letting go of our desires that make us insecure and defensive and worry less about running out of energy. And because we worry less about running out of energy, we become less and less motivated to take energy. We begin stealing energy from each other less and respect and attend to each other more.

You may remember from earlier sections that we can energize ourselves socially in one of two ways. One is by taking energy from other people. The other way is by experiencing unity with other people. During the power struggle and the codependence stage, we have been trying to energize ourselves primarily by taking energy from the other person. When we gradually move toward the stage of mutual respect, we are intuitively realizing that it is easier to energize ourselves by aligning our desires and being mutually respectful (i.e., by experiencing unity with others) rather than taking energy from each other.

This move toward deeper mutual respect is a gradual process. There is no clear-cut line that divides the codependence stage and the stage characterized as deep mutual respect. It is a process of gradually taking less energy from each other and respecting each other more. This process of experiencing deeper mutual respect for each other is a continuous process. There is no endpoint to this process. We can always experience deeper and deeper mutual respect and attend to each other more. The deeper our mutual respect becomes, the more energizing and gratifying our relationship becomes.

As we can see from the explanation above, we move from stability to instability and then gradually move back towards stability until we are even more stable than the state we started out with. It is important to note that not all relationships go through all four stages. Some relationships disintegrate halfway through the process and some remain in the power struggle or codependence stage until the end of the relationship. Although the stages were explained primarily in the context of interpersonal relationships, it may also be applied to situations in which two or more groups (instead of individuals) form and develop relationships.

Dealing with Energy Thieves (The high road)

While we are discussing the realistic aspects of all of this, let's focus on another realistic problem that we encounter quite often in our lives. What do we do when someone is stealing energy from us? We have all been in situations like this and sometimes we wonder what we can do about it. There are no quick fixes for this problem but there are two possible roads we can take to make the best out of this type of unpleasant situation. One is the high road and the other is the human road. Let's examine the high road first. Usually, our natural reaction to this type of situation is not the wisest. When people steal energy from us, we become emotionally hijacked and respond with the fight or flight response. Let's examine these two natural responses.

The first natural reaction we commonly have when someone steals our energy is to become anxious and steal energy right back (i.e., the fight response). However, from what we have learned until now, we know that this may not be the best thing to do. When we steal energy back from someone stealing our energy, we induce more anxiety in the other person and motivate him or her even more to steal energy from us. We must remember that the other person is stealing energy from us because he or she feels low in energy to begin with (thus is motivated to replenish his or her energy). Thus, stealing energy back only feeds the fire of the conflict and often makes the situation even worse.

The other possible natural reaction we have when someone steals energy from us is to escape and avoid the other person so that they cannot continue to steal energy from us (i.e., the flight response). This may be a reasonable response that may benefit us personally in the short run if we no longer intend to continue a relationship with that other person. However, in many cases, we do continue relationships with people who steal energy from us. These people are often important people to us, such as our spouse, our parents, our children, our siblings, our co-workers, or our best friends and we neither want to avoid those people for the rest of our lives nor escape from them every time they steal our energy. We want to develop a positive relationship with them and if we keep avoiding them, we will never be able to do that.

So what should we do? There are two things we should keep in mind. One is to **avoid defensiveness** of any kind as much as possible. When we are defensive, we tune out and shut the other person out. We refuse to allow them to influence us. This is what happens when we steal energy back and this is also what happens when we avoid someone. The key is to do the exact opposite. It is to "open up and allow the other person in". When others steal energy from us, we must remain mindful that the other person really needs our help. Being mindful of this helps us feel like we "want" to help them. It helps us **open up** and **let go of our own desires** and allow the other person to influence us. Remember that we can only lose energy if we don't want the other person to do what he or she is doing (i.e., our desire does not match what is happening). If we let go of our own desires, we can naturally accept the other person and what he or she is doing.

The other thing to keep in mind is to do what we would want the other person to do if we were in the other person's shoes. We often hear the expression "**Lead by example**". This usually means, "Don't tell people what to do or how to do things, just do it the way you think it should be done." If it is actually a very good response, the other person will learn just by observing your behavior and its consequences. They may not pick it up right away, but eventually they will pick it up. We need to be very patient, however, because it takes time for the other person to open up and learn from our leadership. The other person is stealing energy because he or she is depleted and most likely has a thick shell. In order to learn from others, these people will need to make their shells thinner again and this means that they need to resolve their internal conflicts. As we all know, it takes time to resolve of our internal conflicts because we cannot let go of our desires overnight. It is like healing from a painful experience. It takes time for our emotional scars to heal. It may take many many years in some cases.

Why should we refrain from telling others what to do and how to do things? When we tell others what to do or how to do things, we are essentially taking energy from them. No matter how we say it, the underlying message is, "I want you to respect my desire even though I don't respect your desire" and that is exactly what stealing energy is about. And as mentioned earlier, if we steal energy, we motivate the other to steal energy back from us.

If, however, we feel **emotionally hijacked** already, we need to **take a time out** until our hormones in our body subside. This takes at least 30 minutes if not more (it takes time for our hormones to subside). It does seem awkward to take a time out in the middle of an argument but if we do not take it, we go into battle in full force. And although going into battle in full force has its own merits, (as we will see later) the process itself is not very pleasant. Therefore, if there is an alternative that is equally or more effective (like taking a time out), it may be useful to use it. Even if we are not emotionally hijacked, we may want to take a time out if we find that the other person is emotionally hijacked. After taking a time out we could wait for the right time and ask with sincerity what is really on the other person's mind. This is useful sometimes because we often steal energy not because the other person has taken our energy but because something else is bothering us.

The whole idea here is to **transcend one's own selfish desires**. It is what people commonly call "Taking the High Road" or "Being the bigger person" in situations of conflict. Although this may be too idealistic for most of us, this is what we can strive for as much as possible. In trying to become more like this, we may begin to experience states slightly closer to the state of complete transcendence.

Setting Boundaries (The human road)

As most of us probably know from our experiences, taking the high road in conflict situations is much easier said than done. Realistically speaking, most of us are not experiencing states that are even close to transcendence most of the time and we cannot help but feel depleted of energy sometimes in our lives. Because taking the high road may be too difficult for most of us, many psychologists have devised alternative strategies to deal with people who steal energy from us.

In the field of psychotherapy, people often use the term "**setting boundaries**" (e.g., Katherine, 1993; Whitfield, 1993). This refers to our behavior stating, "You can only take this much energy from me. If you take more than that, I will start taking back from you." We intuitively do this to each other so that the other person knows when to stop teasing a friend, when to stop nagging at someone, or when to stop joking around. We often sense people sending us signals (often non-verbal) telling us to back off at a certain point. In this way, we negotiate how much energy we can take and in what ways we can take energy from others in our relationships. Although this is mostly done at a subconscious level we can also do this consciously if someone is stealing energy from us and we are not strong enough to let go of our desires.

The essence of setting boundaries is to **send a message to the other person without stealing energy**. If we steal energy, the other person automatically feels threatened, shuts down (e.g., stops listening), and steals energy back. To do this successfully, we must be honest with ourselves and with others by **noticing and admitting our own insecurities**. When we do this, we make ourselves vulnerable by opening up and expressing our own insecurities but if we are dealing with an important relationship that we wish to improve on, it may be a risk worth taking. The direct expression of insecurities are commonly called, "**I statements**" because we often begin with the word "I". "I am afraid that we will run out of money." "I feel very uncomfortable when the floor is dirty." "I feel sad when you don't call when you are coming home late." "I am sorry but I don't feel strong enough to discuss that now." These statements directly express our own insecurities presenting minimal threat to the other person. In contrast, we should avoid defensive forms of expression accusing the other person. These expressions are called, "**You statements**" because the subject of the statement is typically "You". "You are making me feel inadequate." "Why are you so inconsiderate?" "What is your problem?" "Why can't you keep your room clean?" Using "I statements" instead of "You statements" allows us to express how we truly feel without threatening the other person.

In less threatening cases of others taking energy from us, (i.e., the other person is not too motivated to steal energy from us even though he or she is doing it), it may be enough to gently **change the topic of conversation** to something both people can enjoy, **minimize our responses** indicating non-verbally that we don't want to go there, or just **politely ask them to stop** the behavior. In this way, we are gently taking a little bit of energy back from the other person and sending a subtle warning saying, "I am uncomfortable if you cross this line. Please respect it." This is what the television hero does when he or she is trying to convince the dangerous person to put his or her weapon down and come to peace. The hero makes a gentle gesture to provide others an opportunity to gently step back and let go of their behavior pattern without making them too defensive and motivating them to steal even more energy. Fortunately, most of our conflict situations are not this serious. Therefore if these signs we send are ignored and the other person keeps stealing energy from us, we have the luxury to **politely leave** the other person and escape from the situation or at least take a time-out before we reengage.

If the other person is someone very close to us that we do not want to leave, we must **re-examine our relationship** with him or her and work on it together with that person. This may take considerable effort and time. If we do not want to leave that person, we are most likely dependent on him or her to take energy from as well. In this case, both individuals need to examine themselves and develop more self-awareness of their insecurities and their tendencies to steal energy from the other. This is often a painful and difficult process but it is usually extremely rewarding once it is accomplished to a certain extent. We may have to face things about ourselves that we have been denying and repressing. We may fight with each other about the patterns of stealing energy we have. The relationship may be extremely difficult at certain times during this process. It is important to keep in mind, however, that this is part of the process that leads to personal maturity and a good relationship. It is during this process that we develop a better understanding of ourselves, of the other person, and of the relationship between the two.

Significance of Interpersonal Conflict

As you may have realized from the previous sections, fighting and arguing is not a completely negative thing even if it feels terrible when we are immersed in the process. Most **fighting is a negotiation process**. By fighting, we negotiate the ways we take energy from others and the ways we allow others to take energy from us. By fighting and arguing, we set our boundaries indicating how and how much energy each person can take from each other. We often fight and argue because we cannot agree on the rules of our relationship. We as humans can be insecure, scared, greedy, self-protective, and aggressive. Everyone commonly wants as much as possible and usually, that means we want to take more than we give. This is why we commonly fight when we are making the rules for the relationship. In addition, the more insecure we are, the greedier we become and the more fighting there is. Through all of this, however, it is important to keep in mind that fighting is just part of the process and it will not last forever as long as we learn from these experiences.

In a sense, fighting and arguing is an **opportunity to learn** about the other person, one's own insecurities and internal conflicts, and how they affect our relationship with the other person. Fighting and arguing often happens in the earlier stages of the relationship (Power struggle stage) and also when one person decides to change the rules that were established before because they no longer like those rules for some reason (e.g., a person changes jobs and habitually loses more energy at work than before). As long as we are not completely transcendent, changing the rules and renegotiating and therefore fights and arguments are inevitable in a relationship. Life is constant change. When our circumstances change the dynamics of the relationship often require modification as well. When one person decides to change the rules, we have to renegotiate the rules and this renegotiation may involve some fighting and arguing again.

Sooner or later, if we are patient enough, we reach an agreement and the relationship will become more stable. The more we are willing to learn from the fighting and arguing, the more our relationship develops. Through this process, we often end up learning immensely about the other person, ourselves as well as the relationship between the two. For example, I may learn that I have a certain behavior pattern that is caused by some of my insecurities. By having a fight, I may learn that I am insecure about my relationship with my father and this makes me exploit the insecurities of my spouse by interrogating her whenever she talks about my father. I may also learn that my spouse has a habit of stealing my energy by taking me on a guilt trip about my relationship with my father when she feels depleted of energy. As you can imagine, these insights may be extremely important in improving the quality of our relationship. In contrast, the less we are willing to learn from the fighting and arguing, the less our relationship develops and the more likely we will have similar fights and arguments again in the future. In essence, the fight is not over in these cases. Even though the fight is not over in these cases, we are still progressing slowly. For example, by fighting we may learn that we are not ready for that much of a change yet. Although this may not be the change we wanted, we have still learned something important from the experience.

Overall, this negotiation process may take a few hours or it may take thirty years, just as some conflicts are resolved faster than others. Of course, we sometimes choose not to be patient and give up on the relationship before we come to an agreement. That is our choice. We can try to stick it out or we can let go and move on to another relationship. Either way, we are stuck with both the positive and negative consequences of our choice.

Interpersonal Compatibility

Earlier on, we learned that we form groups with people who have insecurities that are similar to our own. If we look around ourselves, we also notice that we are not only attracted to people with similar insecurities, but we are also attracted to people with the **same amount of insecurity**. People with similar levels of insecurity have patterns of taking similar amounts of energy from each other. A very insecure person habitually takes lots of energy from others whereas a slightly insecure person habitually takes a little energy from others. Thus a man who is very insecure about his gender identity is likely to become friends with other men who are very insecure about their gender identity. A woman who is slightly insecure about her physical appearance is likely to become friends with other women who are slightly insecure about their physical appearance. This allows each person to not only align their desires with each other, but also to **give and take equal amounts of energy** from each other (because the more insecure we are, the more energy we tend to take).

This may make more sense if we interpret this phenomenon using the self-system and the internal conflict model. If I am used to having my brother make degrading and sarcastic remarks at me, I may get to the point where I learn to respond to him by making degrading and sarcastic remarks back at him. My self-system has developed a specific strategy to deal with my brother stealing my energy in this specific way. After a while, I may become so used to this pattern that I feel uncomfortable if my brother does not make degrading and sarcastic remarks at me. At this point, even though it may look like my brother is being hurtful towards me, it may be exactly what I desire. In contrast, my brother may also become so used to my pattern that he also begins to desire having sarcastic remarks made toward him. When this happens, our perceptions have changed and we have now developed a **codependent** relationship. Although we both seem like we are making hurtful sarcastic remarks at each other on the surface, we are actually attending to each other's desires and compensating for each other's insecurities. Because we are compensating for each other's insecurities, we become dependent on each other. We now feel like we need each other so that we can maintain our own patterns.

These patterns transfer onto other relationships as well. Because I have this pattern with my brother now, I may also try this pattern on my peers in school. As you can imagine, I will become friends with those who respond to me like my brother does. These are the people that enable me to maintain my pattern and therefore I am motivated to maintain a relationship with them. On the other hand, the people who do not respond by making degrading and sarcastic remarks back at me do not allow me to maintain my pattern and I am less motivated to maintain a relationship with them. If they make even more degrading and sarcastic remarks than my brother does, I will try to avoid them because I will feel over-stimulated (they take more energy than I am used to). If they make less degrading and sarcastic remarks than my brother does, I will not go out of my way to avoid them because they do not over-stimulate me. However, I will not be particularly attracted to them because they do not provide me with enough stimulation (they take less energy than I am used to). This is why we are more compatible with people who not only have similar insecurities, but also have a similar level of insecurity.

It seems like we can open up and make the outer shells of our self-system thin when we find people who complement our patterns. If someone interacts in a way we are familiar with, we can open up the outer pores of our self-system, regardless of how defensive our specific interpersonal patterns are. This means that we can experience interpersonal unity at a relatively superficial level even if our repertoire of responses in our self-system consist primarily of being defensive and making our shells thick.

From what we have learned, we can conclude that there are **two levels of unity**. The first level of unity is caused by codependence. This type of unity is experienced at a superficial level when our interpersonal patterns complement each other. We discussed earlier that when we have non-matching but compatible desires, we often develop a balanced relationship by giving and receiving equal amounts of energy. This interpersonal experience refers to this superficial type of unity. The second level of unity is a deeper type of unity characterized by mutual attention and respect. This type of unity is experienced at the deep level when it feels like we are simultaneously giving and receiving energy with each other and none of us is losing any energy. It is experienced when things are "clicking" and everything flows naturally. When this occurs, we feel a deep and mysterious sense of oneness with the other person. Figure 15 is an illustration of the difference between the two states of unity. The first type allows only our self-systems to merge and the second type allows us to merge through both our self-systems and our immediate interaction.

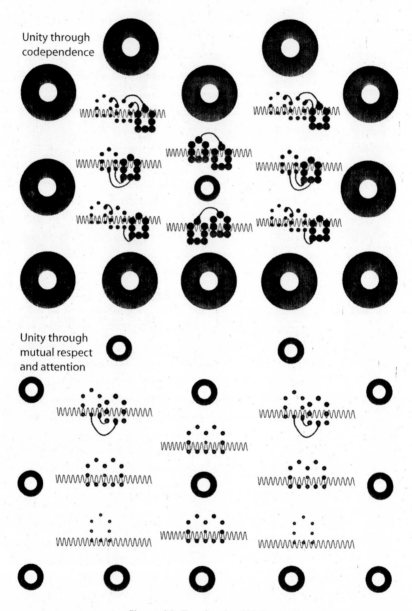

Figure 15. Two levels of Unity

This notion of compatibility through codependence also seems to be the reason why some people like stimulating experiences such as loud and harsh sounding music and shocking art while others like less stimulating experiences like peaceful and calming types of music and art (Sato, Slacum, McGoff, & Murray, 2003). Loud and harsh sounding music and shocking art demands a lot of attention and thus takes lots of energy from us. If we are used to others taking large amounts of energy from us, we tend to like highly stimulating experiences like loud music and shocking art. In contrast, quiet, harmonious, and calming types of music and art demand less attention and thus take less energy from us. If we are used to others taking small amounts of energy from us, we tend to like less stimulating experiences such as peaceful and calming types of music and art. People who are used to others taking small amounts of energy from them like experiences that only take small amounts of energy from them and people who are used to others taking large amounts of energy from them, like experiences that take large amounts of energy from them. The expression, "We like what we are familiar with" seems to apply to a very wide variety of situations.

Natural Motivation to Grow

Many psychologists agree that we all have a **natural motivation to grow**. **Carl Rogers** (1961) for example, states that all humans are born with an **actualizing tendency**, a natural motivation to maintain and enhance not only one's own life but the lives of others as well. **Carl Jung** (1958) has discussed a similar human tendency that he calls **self-realization**. Both of these theorists claim that there is an inner force that drives us to psychologically and spiritually grow and develop into human beings that are increasingly mature. **Abraham Maslow** (1970), another well-known psychologist also claimed that we have a natural tendency to develop. He called this tendency the motivation for **self-actualization**. Self-actualization is commonly defined as a need to live up to one's fullest potential. Given the right circumstances such as water, soil, sunlight and other elements, an acorn has the potential to become a large oak tree. In the same way, given the right circumstances, we as humans have the potential to grow into something psychologically and spiritually wonderful and beautiful. Since humans can develop more conscious awareness as well as more physical mobility than acorns and oak trees, we have some choice in choosing and creating our circumstances (even though there are limitations). This difference in conscious awareness not only leaves us with a need for self-actualization but also makes us consciously strive for it. Regardless of what it is called, these theories have a common theme. Given the right circumstances, we will grow and mature as human beings.

Another common and important assumption of many developmental theories is that we all grow one step at a time and we can only make certain kinds of progress when we are ready for it. Those of us who are familiar with the developmental theories of Piaget and Inhelder (1969), Freud (1966), Erikson (1963, 1968, 1978), and Levinson (1978), know that all of them discuss development as an invariant sequence of numerous stages. The notion that development occurs in an invariant sequence of stages assumes that we develop one step at a time and that certain types of development are only possible when we have reached a certain stage.

These two points discussed above have **two important implications**. The first implication is that we do not need to "make" people grow. We do not even have to "make" ourselves grow. We often become concerned that people around us are not making the developmental strides that we expect and often end up feeling frustrated trying to "make" them grow. The fact that all of us have this natural motivation and the belief that people will make certain important developments when they are ready gives us hope that we ourselves, as well as people around us, want to and will most likely grow without any pressure from the outside. Being mindful of this helps us remain patient and hopeful that people (including ourselves) will learn and grow whenever they (or we) are ready, regardless of whether we worry about it or not. The second implication reinforces a point already made earlier. It is that creating the right circumstances for people to grow (including ourselves) is beneficial to all of us. All of this suggests that although we are typically more concerned about "making" people grow we should be more concerned about providing a caring environment that is conducive to natural growth and maturation.

Development as Decrease in Egocentrism

What does it mean to grow? We all know that people develop in different directions and this is partly what makes each of us unique. Many psychologists, however, suggest that there are some commonalities in the way we develop. We discussed earlier how our self-system grows into a system of understanding that is **more inclusive of a wider variety of situations**. Many developmental theories are consistent in that respect (e.g., Piaget & Inhelder, 1969; Kohlberg, 1981, Gilligan, 1982). One factor that causes our self-system to be more inclusive of a wider variety of situations is the **increase in awareness of other people's needs and desires**. As we develop, we become increasingly aware that we are not the only ones who have needs and desires. Furthermore, the more we develop, the more we consider the needs and desires of an increasingly wider range of people. We begin our lives focusing on, "what is best for myself". Then we move toward, "what is best for myself and the person I am directly interacting with right now". Then we begin to focus more on, "what is best for my family". Later on this may turn into, "what is best for my community" and then, "what is good for my nation" and this goes on and on. Piaget and Inhelder (1969) have discussed how young children are **egocentric** in their views and motivations. They are unable to see things from another person's perspective. When they become older they become less egocentric and begin understanding that their views, needs, and desires are sometimes different from those of others. As we become less egocentric, we become more group-centric of increasingly larger groups. Various theorists on moral development have discussed this notion in great detail (e.g., Kohlberg, 1981; Gilligan, 1982).

Lawrence Kohlberg (1981) for instance, discusses how moral development progresses through three levels. When we are in the first level, known as the **preconventional level**, what is good and bad is largely determined by our own personal needs and desires. If something satisfies my desires, it is good. If it prevents them from being satisfied, it is bad. This understanding of the world roughly corresponds to the egocentric child discussed earlier. When we move to the second level of moral development, known as the **conventional level**, we become more concerned about the views, needs, and desires of others. At the beginning of this level, we are mostly concerned about what other people think about us. If others approve of the behavior (i.e., it satisfies the desires of others), then it is perceived as morally good. If others disapprove (i.e., it does not satisfy the desires of others), then it is perceived as bad. Here we see that we now are concerned with the desires and needs of specific others in addition to our own needs and desires. In a later stage of the same level, we beginning developing an understanding that rules and laws exist for the sake of social order. Therefore we must abide by the rules if we want to prevent social chaos. Here we see the development of concern for more than the people we directly interact with. At the third and final level of morality, known as the **postconventional level**, we find that conventional laws and the general social system are not always respectful of all individuals. This leads us to develop our own individual sense of morality that is respectful of even a wider variety of individuals than conventional laws and the present social system.

Moreover, **Carol Gilligan** (1982), another scholar of human development, developed her own theory of **moral development in women** because she believed that Kohlberg's theory applies primarily to men. Gilligan suggested that because women focus on relationships more than men do, they progress through three different stages of moral development. The first stage, known as **"Orienta-**

tion to individual survival" is very similar to Kohlberg's preconventional level except that it is focused on contrasting one's own needs and desires against the needs and desires of others. In this stage, the needs and desires of the individual self is more important than those of others. Therefore, what is good for me is what is good in general, even if it is not good for others. In the second stage called **"Goodness as self-sacrifice"**, we begin believing that it is morally good to sacrifice our own desires and needs to satisfy the needs and desires of other people. In this stage, what is good for others is what is good in general, even if it is not good for me. Finally in the last stage known as **"Morality of nonviolence"**, we slowly stop seeing things as "my needs and desires" versus "your needs and desires" and begin viewing things as "our needs and desires". In this stage it is no longer a question of what is good for whom. The focus is on what is good for all of us involved and my desire becomes what "we" want rather than what "I" want. In fact, in this stage what "I" want becomes what is best for everyone involved. Although the details of the theories differ, it is clear that there is a common core in the developmental theories discussed above. The more we develop, the less self-centered or group-centered we become. As we develop, we continuously learn to consider the needs and desires of a wider range of people.

Helping others Grow

Oftentimes, we are placed in positions in life where we would like to help other people grow, whether it is as a parent, older sibling, teacher, health care provider, provider of job training, or even just as a friend. Although people have suggested a variety of ways to help other people grow, they can be organized on a **spectrum of forcefulness**. Some methods of helping others grow are extremely forceful while others are much less forceful. Let's begin by examining the more forceful methods.

The highly **forceful methods** require us to aggressively **break down the self-system** of the other person. In order to do this, we do certain things so that their self-system does not allow them to maintain their energy. We intervene with so much force that the person can no longer keep repeating his or her undesirable patterns that were reflective of his or her self-system. This is what we do when we confront people denying their life threatening addiction to drugs. This is what drill sergeants do in boot camps. This is what we do when we force an abuse victim to leave her abusive spouse. The extremely forceful methods are commonly considered to be the last option when we face people who are either extremely dangerous to others or in extreme danger themselves. In essence, the forceful way requires us to break down the other person's thick shell around the self-system and influence the self-system to change.

Once the shell is broken down and the self-system is significantly influenced, however, we must provide the person some support so that he or she can develop a new self-system with more desirable patterns on his or her own. This is the essence of "**tough love**". We are tough when we break down the other person's self-system, but we are supportive when the other person struggles to create a new self-system on his or her own afterwards. This is what we do in drug rehabilitation clinics. We don't merely deprive them from the drugs. We support them during the recovery process[4]. It is clear that this point has an important implication on interpersonal ethics. It suggests that we should not break down the self-system of other people if we are not willing to support them during their struggles to rebuild a new self-system. Even though we often rationalize that we are trying to help, breaking down other people's self-systems without supporting them in the rebuilding process is nothing more than stealing energy.

As you may know from personal experience, the forceful way is often unsuccessful. A proverb of the Lakota native North American tribe translates, "Force, no matter how concealed, begets resistance." When we force people to change their ways, they change temporarily only because they are being forced to, not because they want to. Therefore, they revert back to their old ways as soon as we stop enforcing the new behavior. This is commonly referred to as **first order change** (Watzlawick, Weakland, & Fisch, 1974). It is a superficial form of change that is caused by the stealing of energy. The person changing feels controlled and is only behaving differently for superficial reasons. In this case, the self-system is resisting influence and does not change much. In most cases, this type of change is not the type of change we are hoping for. When we want others to change, we often want them to mature and develop as human beings. We want them to be intrinsically motivated (i.e., motivated from within) and not extrinsically motivated (i.e., motivated by external forces) to be different.

However, sometimes the forceful way does create lasting change. For the forceful way to work, the individual being forced to change needs to restructure his or her understanding of the new patterns. We must see the change as **something we desire and not as something other people desire**. This cognitive restructuring often occurs when we experience **cognitive dissonance**, a state in which our behaviors do not match our attitudes (Festinger, 1957). For example, let's assume that other people force me to do some community service. Although I initially perceive this as others stealing energy from me, it feels disempowering to think that I am forced to do something. In order to feel empowered, I change my perception of the event and think that I am doing this community service because I desire it and not because I am being forced to do it. When this occurs, I keep behaving in the new way even when I am no longer forced to do it. This type of change is the result of breaking down and then restructuring the self-system. This is what is commonly referred to as second order change (Watzlawick, Weakland, & Fisch, 1974). Second order change is the process of **changing** the contents of "**my desire**" in my internal conflict. Instead of making my desire fight against what has, is, or could happen, I change my desire so that it matches what has, is, or could happen. In sum, the weakness of the forceful method is that as long as this restructuring of the self-system does not occur, we eventually revert back to our old ways, even if we are forced to change our behaviors temporarily.

As mentioned earlier, some methods of helping others grow are extremely forceful and others are much less forceful. Let's shift our focus and examine the less forceful and more **patient ways** to help people grow. The patient way assumes that people have a natural motivation to grow and that they will develop whenever they are ready. These methods focus on **providing a safe, accepting, caring, and respectful environment** so that people feel comfortable and courageous enough to face their own insecurities caused by their internal conflicts and figure out a way to resolve those internal conflicts on their own. The more accepting and respectful the people around us are, the safer we feel to **face our own insecurities**. Facing our own insecurities is the first step in resolving the internal conflicts that are causing those insecurities. Furthermore, resolving those internal conflicts is the same as **making our shells thinner** and enabling us to float higher in the ocean[5]. As the label "the patient way" implies, this is often a time-consuming process because we only face our own insecurities when we are naturally ready.

Client-centered therapy, a form of therapy originated by **Carl Rogers** (1951), is a classic example of the patient way to help others grow. Client-centered therapy focuses on providing a safe, accepting, caring, and respectful environment so that the client feels safe and courageous enough to face his or her own insecurities. Rogers states that there are three important ingredients in providing the safe and caring environment necessary for client-centered therapy. The first is that the therapist must provide the client with **unconditional positive regard**. As discussed earlier, unconditional positive regard is the idea that we love, accept, and respect others for just being themselves regardless of who they are and what they do. The second ingredient is that the therapist must provide the client with **empathic understanding**. Empathic understanding is showing that the therapist is interested in the client and understands how the client feels. Empathic understanding is different from plain old listening. We often feel frustrated when others are listening to us halfheartedly while they are watching television or reading the newspaper and say, "You are not listening to me!" In many cases, they have heard what we have said but they are not showing that they care and understand how we feel. In this case, there are listening but there is a lack of empathic understanding. As you can imagine, we are much more likely to feel comfortable and courageous to face our own insecurities when the other person is empathically understanding us than when the other person is listening halfheartedly. The third ingredient in client-centered therapy is that the therapist must be experiencing **congruence**. As discussed earlier, congruence is when our desires match what has, is, or could happen. This means that, in order for client-centered therapists to be effective, they must feel relatively secure emotionally and experience minimal levels of internal conflict. As you can imagine, it would be very difficult for an insecure and internally conflicted person to provide an environment of unconditional positive regard for others.

Dealing with narrow mindedness of one's own Groups

Sometimes, it is not another individual we want to help change but our own group. We learned earlier that we have a tendency to form groups with people who have similar insecurities. Because many people in a group may have similar insecurities, we often end up with a larger insecure unit, the insecure group. Just as insecurities make an individual narrow minded, insecurity of groups creates narrow mindedness in groups. **Irving Janis** (1982) examined this interesting phenomenon and characterized it as **groupthink**. Groupthink is a phenomenon that causes us to become narrow minded for the sake of group unity. In these situations, we ignore any information inconsistent with the needs and desires of one's own group. In his work, Janis outlined numerous characteristics of groupthink. The first characteristic is an **illusion of invulnerability** of one's own group. To compensate for our insecurities, we convince ourselves that our group is special and that nothing negative can happen to our group. The second characteristic is an **unquestioned belief of the correctness of the group's desires**. We deal with our insecurities convincing ourselves that whatever we decide is correct by ignoring any disconfirming evidence. The third characteristic is **rationalization**. If for some reason, we are faced with evidence disconfirming the uniquely positive qualities and correctness of the group's desires and decisions, we engage in rationalization so that the evidence no longer seems valid. The fourth characteristic is **conformity pressure**. All of the members of the group feel pressure to agree with the leader and the majority of the group. The fifth characteristic is that there are **mindguards** in the group. Certain members of the group take the role of censoring any information inconsistent with the desires of the group. They make sure that the majority of individuals in the group are not exposed to evidence disconfirming the uniquely positive qualities and correctness of the group's desires and decisions. If we use the ocean analogy to understand groupthink, it is as if the group is one unit. In addition, instead of having an individual with a thick shell, we have a group with a thick shell.

Just as some individuals may be more insecure than others, some groups are more insecure than others. However, because no group is free of insecurities, the characteristics of groupthink are observable in all groups. This phenomenon is often overlooked in our own groups because it is difficult to examine our own groups objectively. In order to **minimize groupthink**, Janis makes a number of suggestions. One thing we could do is to assign a **devil's advocate** so that at least one person feels free to express his or her concerns regarding the correctness of their decisions and desires of the group in general. Another thing Janis suggests is to solicit and welcome the critiques of **outside experts**. This minimizes the possibility of groups ignoring information inconsistent with their agenda. Another suggestion is to **subdivide the group into smaller groups** for discussions and examine the differences between the conclusions of the smaller groups. This is especially useful when some people feel uncomfortable expressing their concerns to a large group of individuals or a specific individual in the larger group. The last suggestion is to call a **second-chance meeting** to air any lingering doubts and encourage critical evaluation before any important decisions are implemented. This legitimizes the expression of doubts and criticisms among the group members since it is defined as the purpose of the meeting.

Dealing with Intergroup Conflict

Insecurity of a group can also lead to intergroup conflict. Intergroup conflict is similar to interpersonal conflict because in both cases, two parties are competing for energy. In interpersonal conflict, we have two or more individuals competing for energy. In intergroup conflict, we have two or more groups competing for energy. Because intergroup conflict is something we are faced with almost every day in our lives, researchers have examined various methods of resolving it. The two most commonly discussed ways to resolve intergroup conflict involve an impartial "third party" member (Rubin, Pruitt, & Kim, 1994). The third party member must be someone who does not have any interest in what any of the groups may gain or lose. The first of these methods is known as **arbitration**. It is when a third party member objectively examines the conflict and determines who should receive what. Examples of this type of conflict resolution method can be observed in the legal system. Arbitration is what judges and juries engage in when they are in court. Parents also sometimes function as arbitrators when they encounter conflict among groups of siblings. One of the disadvantages of arbitration is that it does not always lead to satisfaction on both sides. This implies that the conflict is sometimes not completely resolved even after arbitration. The other method to resolve intergroup conflict using a third party member is known as **mediation**. With mediation, a third party member, known as the mediator, takes turns discussing the situation with each group separately. Because the group members are not directly faced with the opposing group, this method minimizes the defensiveness of the group members when they are communicating about the desires of their own as well as those of the other group. This method is known to be very effective in facilitating the process of giving and receiving when two groups are in conflict. Although this method is more time consuming than arbitration, mediation is more likely to lead to satisfaction of both groups (leading to a true resolution of the conflict).

Sometimes we are faced with intergroup conflict and there is no impartial third party to be the arbitrator or mediator. What do we do then? Although there are many possibilities **Charles Osgoode** (1962) has suggested a very interesting and effective way to deal with situations of this kind. His resolution method is known as **GRIT** (an abbreviation for Graduated and Reciprocal Initiatives in Tension Reduction). Osgoode maintains that the key characteristic of intergroup conflict is that the groups involved **feel threatened** by the other group(s) in some way. Therefore, in order to resolve the conflict, we must decrease whatever is threatening to the other groups. GRIT provides a framework to **deescalate the conflict** by decreasing what is threatening to the other groups. The framework is the following. One group begins by initiating a few small deescalatory actions with conciliatory intent (e.g., putting our weapons down, doing the other group a favor, smiling) and invites the other group to reciprocate. The other group reciprocates with the same amount of deescalatory action or may make a few more small deescalatory actions and invites the other to reciprocate. If the other group merely reciprocates, the initiator makes a few more small deescalatory actions and invites the other group to reciprocate again. If the other group makes a few more small deescalatory actions, the initiator then reciprocates and makes a few more small deescalatory actions and invites the other to reciprocate again. In this way we gradually decrease what is threatening to each other little by little until we find each other no longer threatening. When we reach a point where the groups are no longer threatening to each other, the intergroup conflict disappears. If we examine GRIT using the ocean analogy, it is as if we are taking turns lifting each other up little by little until we are both well above the water. This enables us to feel safe and make our shells thinner again.

You may have noticed that all of these methods of resolving **intergroup conflict** apply to **interpersonal conflict** as well. Moreover, although all of these methods were primarily explained using two groups, they can all be applied to situations involving more than two groups in conflict. They can also be applied to situations involving more than two individuals in conflict as well. Therefore, it may be useful to keep some of these things in mind when we experience situations of social conflict in the future.

Consciousness

Subjective and Objective Experiences and the Cycle of Life

People often differentiate experiences using the terms subjective and objective. We all have an intuitive understanding of what these terms mean, but what is the basis for this differentiation? The basis for this differentiation is in our natural thought processes (Sartre, 1957). When I think, "My shoulder is bothering me" I have separated myself from my shoulder. Grammatically speaking, "my shoulder" is the subject and the "me" is the object. From the perspective of consciousness, "me" is the subject and "my shoulder" is the object. Although my shoulder is part of me, I have created a boundary between "me" and "my shoulder" in my mind. This is the root of the **subject-object differentiation**. When something is experienced objectively, it is experienced as something separate from the self. When something is experienced subjectively, it is experienced not as separate from the self. It is something intuitive directly based on sensations and feelings. It is directly experienced as a part of the self (i.e., subject).

This differentiation between subject and object is extremely important in understanding the development of consciousness. As discussed earlier, there are many levels of consciousness that correspond to various levels of human development. In the beginning of life, most things are experienced as one subjective blob. There is minimal differentiation between the subject and object. This lack of differentiation is commonly used to explain why very young infants tend to see a black and white checkerboard as one general blob of gray (Banks, 1980). As we grow up, we differentiate more and more throughout our lives. We begin by differentiating object from subject. This is the beginning of what we traditionally consider "conscious awareness". It is the also the basis of thought and primitive forms of language. Soon after we begin differentiating objects from the subject, we begin differentiating objects from other objects. Not only do I separate my shoulder from my self, I also separate my shoulder from my elbow. These differentiations enable us to become "thinking" beings. This is what **Piaget** and

Inhelder (1969) describe as the process of moving through the **sensorimotor** and **preoperational stages** in cognitive development.

A little later in our childhood, we develop the ability to think about thinking. At this stage, we not only separate objects from the subject, we can also separate what used to be the subject and make that into an object as well. Before this stage, I could separate the object from the subject but I could not think about myself separating the object from the subject. In this new stage, I can think about myself differentiating the subject from the object. This is the primary characteristic of what Piaget and Inhelder (1969) called the **concrete operational stage**. As we move through our life, we eventually arrive at a stage where we develop the ability to think about ourselves thinking about thinking. At this stage, we not only are able to think about separating objects from the subject, we also are able to separate what used to be the subject (i.e., myself thinking about separating objects from the subject) and make that into an object as well. This is the primary characteristic of what Piaget and Inhelder (1969) called the **formal operational stage** in cognitive development. Figure 16 is an illustration of this process of development. The transition from level 1 to level 2 in Figure 16 occurs during the sensorimotor and the preoperational stage. The concrete operational stage marks the beginning of consciousness at level 3. The formal operational stage marks the beginning of consciousness at level 4.

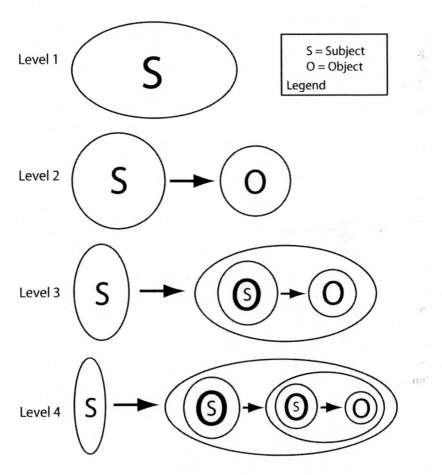

Figure 16. The Development of Consciousness

In sum, the more we mature, the more we develop the ability to step out of ourselves and see ourselves more and more from an objective standpoint. Earlier, we discussed that the more we mature, the more we are able to consider and respect the desires and needs of a wider range of people. The development of consciousness explains exactly why this happens. From what was discussed above, we could say that the more we mature, the more self-awareness we develop. The more self-awareness we develop, the better we are able to understand our own existence in relation to everyone around us. The better we are able to understand our own existence in relation to everyone around us, the more we are able to consider and respect the desires and needs of a wider range of people. Although

Piaget and Inhelder (1969) refer to this as cognitive development, modern developmental scholars commonly refer to this as socio-emotional (or moral) development.

As we can see from above, more maturity means **more awareness**. If we take this one step further, we find that more awareness means more freedom. For example, let us say that I have recently developed awareness that I use the interrogation behavior pattern to steal energy from my sister. I am now able to think about my thinking. Before I had this awareness, I just automatically reacted by stealing energy in that way without consciously thinking about it. Now that I am aware of my pattern, I have the freedom of choice to keep using this pattern or to change it. This is why awareness leads to freedom. The more aware we become, the less we are confined by our subconscious patterns of thought and behavior. Freedom, however, has its price. The more freedom we have, the more we feel responsible for what we do. If I interrogate my sister without being aware of the fact that I am stealing her energy, I along with everyone around me would feel that I am less responsible for my actions. As long as I am not aware of it, I can rationalize my actions and think, "I am doing this to help my sister develop." Moreover, the people around me would probably just think, "He has annoying habits but his intentions are good." However, if I choose to steal energy by interrogating my sister even after I become aware of this pattern, I as well as everyone around me would feel that I am cruel and should be responsible for my actions. As is evident in this example, the **more freedom** we have, the **more responsible** we must be.

Unfortunately, however, we often find this responsibility to be an unbearable burden and refuse to mature and develop because we are afraid of taking responsibility for our actions (Fromm, 1941). The fact that we all **blame others** for many things in our lives is evidence for this. We blame other people, we blame our circumstances, and we blame certain events in our lives to escape from taking responsibility for our behaviors, our development, and our happiness. By blaming other people and things, we **are refusing to develop** our awareness of how we relate to the world. By blaming others, we **escape the responsibility** to improve any situation. The more awareness we develop, the more responsible we feel for improving various situations. As long as we don't mature and develop our awareness, we can keep repeating the same problematic patterns that we are accustomed to without changing and without feeling responsible for them. It is an easy way out in the short run but confines us in a state of arrested development in the long run.

Figure 17 is an illustration of this maturation process discussed above. As we can see in this figure, we experience a state of complete subjective unity before we exist as humans. As we begin our lives, we experience more and more things as separate from our selves. This is the process of differentiating objects from the subject. Soon after that, we also begin differentiating those objects from other objects as well. As you can see in Figure 17, this process of differentiating the objects from the subject makes the objects take increasingly more space and leaves the subject increasingly less space. This corresponds to the process of **becoming increasing aware of what we used to experience as the subject**. My increase in awareness about my pattern of stealing energy by interrogating my sister would be an example of becoming increasingly aware of what used to be experienced as the subject. Before I developed that awareness, my pattern was only subjectively experienced and therefore I was unable to objectively think about it. I was just responding at an intuitive level (like many animals do) and I was not consciously aware of the process. Now I am able to consciously think about it because I have separated it from my subjective self and made it an object. As we mature, more and more things that were initially experienced subjectively become objectively experienced. In addition to this, maturation also involves the development of a conscious understanding of the relationships between many of the things we experience. This corresponds to the integration of objects with other objects. Finally, according to some theorists, the ideal endpoint called complete transcendence is a state in which the subject becomes so small that it disappears (e.g., Watts, 1966; Wilber, 1970). It is a point where everything is the object. Remember, however, that the object can only exist when there is a subject because the very definition of an object is that it is something experienced as separate from the subject. Since there is no subject in this final state of mind, it is commonly referred to as a state in which everything is experienced as the subject.

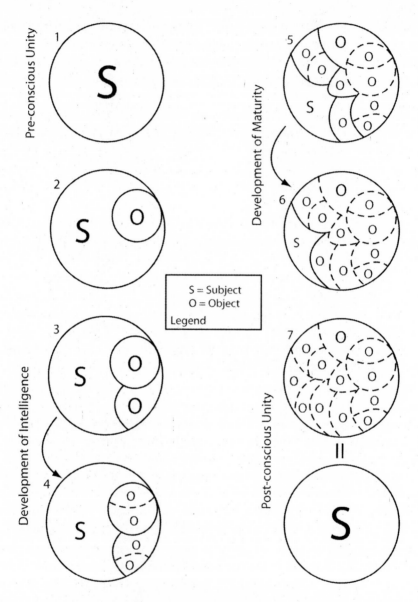

Figure 17. The Cycle of Life

It is interesting to note that there are **two general processes** occurring during life. One process is the simultaneous process of separating the object from the subject and integrating a part of what used to be the subject with other objects (i.e., understanding our existence in relation to others). During this process, we begin to identify more and more with the object by integrating more and more of what used to be the subject with the object. This process enables us to see an increasingly bigger picture of how we exist in relation to others. As a consequence, this process helps us exist in more harmonious unity with other people and things. This process is what leads to true maturity or socio-emotional development as defined by various scholars (e.g., Gilligan, 1982; Goleman, 1995; Kohlberg, 1981). Eventually, if we reach a state of complete transcendence, we differentiate everything from the subject (so that the subject disappears) and integrate all objects with other objects and we experience objective unity. However, since objects cannot exist without a subject, we commonly call it subjective unity instead of objective unity. In sum, we begin by venturing out of subjective unity into the world of conflict between subject and object and then we end by returning back to subjective unity. Therein lies the beauty in the cycle of our lives. It is like a story with a peaceful beginning, conflict and excitement in the middle, and then a peaceful ending after the climax. This is probably why Black Elk, the well-known wise man of the Lakota native North American tribe says, "The life of a man is a circle from childhood to childhood, and so it is in everything where power moves" (Black Elk & Lyon, 1991).

The other process involves identifying with the subject and differentiating objects into smaller and smaller categories. This process has many important implications for physical survival and reproduction. Firstly, it helps us escape danger. Knowing the difference between a rattlesnake and a garden snake is helpful to survival. Knowing the difference between the gas pedal and brake pedal in my car is helpful to survival. Secondly this process helps us control and manipulate things in the environment to help us survive. It helps us create better clothing and shelter, find ways to obtain resources such as food and other energy sources, as well as develop technology and strategies useful to accomplish these things. Knowing the difference between brick and mud, cotton and wool, trucks and tractors, method A and method B helps us accomplish these things more efficiently. This process is often referred to as the development of intelligence (see Figure 17). However, this process is also what makes us experience internal conflict. For example, at first I may not differentiate brand A from brand B and am therefore happy as long as I have either brand. After a while, I differentiate brand A from brand B and decide that brand A is more useful than brand B. I now feel internal conflict when I get brand B. What I desire (i.e., brand A) does not match what is happening (i.e., I am getting brand B). Therefore, the more we differentiate objects in our minds, the more potential we have for internal conflict.

Carl Jung (1958) studied these two processes and suggested that the latter process occurs more than the former process in the **first phases of life**. In the first phases of life, we focus on what Jung calls "**individuation**". Individuation refers to the differentiation of objects. During this time, we are primarily focused on controlling and manipulating things in the environment so that we are able to survive and reproduce. It is a period of life primarily focused on taking as well as protecting our energy from the environment. Because of this, there is more potential for internal conflict during these periods. Perhaps this is why the early phases of life such as adolescence and early adulthood are typically the most active and tumultuous times in our lives. In the **later phases of life**, the former process occurs more than the latter. This makes us less concerned about things related to physical survival and reproduction, and more concerned about understanding our existence in relation to everything and everyone else. During this time of life, we concentrate on energizing ourselves through unity and harmony. This is the process behind developing a self-system that considers the needs and desires of an increasingly wider range of people and things in nature. Jung calls this process "**transcendence**" and it is commonly associated with the concept of socio-emotional development or just plain becoming mature as a human being. Thus although the early signs of this type of development in our consciousness can be observed in childhood and adolescence (Piaget & Inhelder, 1969), its full manifestation seems to occur largely in the later parts of life (Jung, 1958). The transition between these two phases of life is often considered to be the essence of the mid-life transition. The more we experience difficulty making the transition from the process focusing on intelligence, survival, and reproduction to the process focusing on developing maturity and experiencing harmony, the more we tend to experience something that could be commonly characterized as a "**mid-life crisis**" (Levinson, 1978).

Digital and Analog modes of Consciousness

Various scholars discuss how humans have two general modes of functioning. Although some call the two modes, **digital** and **analog** (e.g., Walter, 1994, Watzlawick, Beavin, & Jackson, 1967), whereas others call them **analytical** and **holistic** (e.g., Nisbett, Peng, Choi, & Norenzayan, 2001), the distinction is very similar. The digital (or analytical) mode of consciousness is the part of us that separates. This mode of functioning is largely responsible for the formation of boundaries in our mind. It makes us separate subject from object, objects from different objects, one procedure from another procedure, one experience from another experience (such as digital and analog), as well as my desires from what has, is, or could happen. As we can see, the digital mode of functioning is the source of internal conflict but there is much more to this mode of functioning. Because it helps us differentiate our self from non-self, it is a mode of functioning necessary for our tendency for self-definition and self-preservation regardless of how the self is defined (i.e., as an individual physical entity, individual self-system, individual and his of her belongings, or a group of people, etc.). Furthermore, because this mode of functioning allows us to categorize experiences and separate events as causes and effects, it is the basis for logical reasoning and **goal-oriented** thinking. These functions roughly correspond to the general functions of the **left cerebral hemisphere** for most right-handed people (Gazzinaga, 1995).

The other mode of functioning is commonly called the analog (or holistic) mode. This mode of consciousness is the part of us that integrates. It is the part of us that puts things together so that we can experience the larger whole. It is this mode of functioning that allows us to integrate objects with objects so that we can see things as a larger whole. For example, when we look at someone's nose, we immediately identify it as a nose without even thinking of the different parts that make up the nose. We don't divide the nose into the left half and the right half or into individual cells that make up the nose. We see it and just think, "nose". When we sing a song, we do not think of each sound we make every moment as separate sounds. We think of the whole song (or a phrase) as one continuous piece. That is what the analog mode of functioning does. It integrates things spatially and temporally so that we don't experience things as many separate parts put together but as one whole thing. It allows us to experience things in relation to each other. The analog mode of functioning is also what allows us to experience things subjectively without separating the objects from the subject. Socially, this is what allows us to see things as "us" rather than "you" versus "me". It is also what allows us be more **process-oriented** rather than goal-oriented, and because of this, it is the part of us that enables us to experience "Flow". When we experience "Flow" one moment naturally flows into the other with no sense of separation between those moments. This mode of functioning allows us to experience balance, harmony, and beauty since balance, harmony, and beauty are based on how things relate to one another to form a larger whole. These functions roughly correspond to the general functions of the **right cerebral hemisphere** for most right-handed people (Gazzinaga, 1995).

Because we are "conscious" beings, we cannot avoid separating objects from the subject. However, at the same time, we cannot avoid experiencing things subjectively either. Furthermore, because larger wholes are made up of smaller wholes and those smaller wholes are made of even smaller wholes and this can continue infinitely, everything is a "whole" at some level. This implies that we cannot avoid experiencing things as wholes. Therefore it may be quite safe to assume that we are almost never completely in one mode of operation. Every experience is made of a combination of the digital and analog mode of functioning.

There may be individual differences concerning which mode we use more in general. Although it may not be as simple as the differences between "right brained" and "left brained" people typically portrayed in popular magazines, the people who use the analog mode more often (typically called "right brained") tend to value **subjective experiences** and may seem **spontaneous** and **intuitive**. These people are typically attracted to the subjective beauty of the **arts** and **humanities**. In contrast, the people who use the digital mode more often (typically called "left brained") tend to value **objective experiences** and may seem to be more **logical** and **analytical**. These people are typically attracted to the objective beauty of the natural **sciences**.

Archetypes of Femininity & Masculinity

The digital and analog modes of functioning are commonly associated with the archetypical images of masculinity and femininity (Bakan, 1966; Jung, 1936). Although both males and females have both masculine and feminine aspects to some extent, certain characteristics are considered to be masculine and certain other ones are considered to be feminine because the majority of one sex has more of a certain tendency than the other. On the one hand, the archetypical image of **femininity** is commonly associated with **analog** characteristics. It is associated with the emphasis on subjective experiences such as an emphasis on the **emotional quality** of our experiences. Moreover, it is associated with focusing on the **experiential process** rather than the end goal. It is also associated with things **fluid and continuous**, such as relationships among things, beauty and harmony, the rhythmic nature of giving and receiving, the continuous flow of life by giving birth. This is perhaps why nature and earth are considered female in most cultures. Even in the English language, we use expressions like "mother nature" and "mother earth". This is also perhaps why women are generally considered to be more "relational" in nature in most cultures. This analog tendency that makes us integrate things into larger wholes may also be one of the reasons why more women have the tendency to simultaneously use both cerebral hemispheres of the brain more than men (Kimura, 1999).

Men on the other hand have more of a tendency to separate the two cerebral hemispheres and use one cerebral hemisphere more than the other for any given task. This is perhaps reflective of the **digital** nature of the **masculinity** archetype. Masculinity is commonly associated with things that are separate such as the tendency to objectify our experiences and the tendency to experience things as competing rather than functioning together as one. Furthermore, because it is associated with **separation** and **competition**, it is also associated with **internal conflict**. If we take one more step in our associations, we notice why masculinity is often associated with physical and social power. The concept of **power** is associated with separating the object from the subject and making the subject win over the object. Masculinity is also associated with the emphasis on perceiving things as **cause and effect**, which requires the separation of events in time, another common digital function. Because of this emphasis on cause and effect, masculinity is often associated with focusing on the **end goal** rather than the experiential process. While the masculine aspect of us separates our tasks into separate things and motivates us to finish one thing after another, the feminine aspect of us allows us to enjoy and appreciate the process of actually engaging in the tasks. Perhaps because of this masculine tendency to focus on the end, males in almost all cultures tend to have a shorter life expectancy, higher infant mortality, and higher suicide rate. As Freud (1966) suggested, although death is something we typically want to avoid, death can also be regarded as the end goal of life.

Cultural Differences in Consciousness

As we will see in this section, this distinction between digital and analog modes of functioning is important in understanding not only the concepts of masculinity and femininity but also cultural differences as well. Geert Hofstede (1980) examined many people in a large variety of different cultures and found that a variable known as **individualism-collectivism** is one of the most useful variables in examining many of the prominent differences among cultures in this world. Since then, Harry Triandis (1995) systematically examined the characteristics of various cultures that lie on various points of the individualism-collectivism continuum. Triandis suggested that compared to individualistic cultures, people in collectivistic cultures tend to pay more attention to the groups they belong to rather than the self as an individual. He elaborated on the characteristics of the cultures that are considered to be highly individualistic and the cultures that are considered to be highly collectivistic in great detail. The following is a brief out-line of his findings.

Although all cultures vary in their levels of individualism and collectivism, countries such as the **United States, Canada, United Kingdom, Australia**, as well as some of the countries in northwestern Europe are considered to have highly individualistic cultures. In contrast, highly collectivistic cultures are gener-ally found in **Asia, Africa, and South America**. Collectivistic cultures emphasize the strict use of **social norms** and **detailed scripts** of how one should behave in a large variety of situations. For example, in Japan (a highly collectivistic culture) there are strict rules about how and when to bow depending on whom we are bowing to and who else is with us. Social rules and scripts are very important in collectivistic cultures because people function more as a group. In order to func-tion harmoniously as a group, people need to cooperate and work in relation to others. Having rules and scripts about how to behave helps them figure out how to cooperate with each other so that the group can function effectively. In a col-lectivistic culture, the most important unit is the group and not the individual. Many times, people may sacrifice their individual benefits for the **benefits of the group** in these cultures.

In contrast, highly individualistic cultures emphasize **personal preferences and benefits**. The rules and scripts about how one should behave in these cul-tures are much less restrictive. In highly individualistic cultures, people tend to focus on their personal desires rather than rules involving their behaviors. This is because personal benefits are generally considered to be more important than group benefits in these cultures. In sum, the more collectivistic a culture, the more people focus on "what am I expected to do in this situation" and the more individualistic a culture, the more people focus on "what do I want to do in this situation".

This sounds like people in collectivistic cultures are more considerate and experience more unity with others than people in individualistic cultures. As pre-viously discussed, however, although feeling that we belong to a group allows us to feel more secure and stable, it can also be the root of **intergroup conflict** char-acterized by narrow mindedness, prejudice, and mob mentality. Because of this, collectivistic cultures also have a higher tendency for **narrow mindedness** and **prejudice**. This leads to the tendency of people in collectivistic cultures to be very caring toward ingroup members but very cruel toward outgroup members. In addition to this, the more collectivistic a culture, the more emphasis there is on **social hierarchy**. This means that there is a greater difference in social power between people who are at the high end and people at the low end of the social hierarchy in a collectivistic culture. Hofstede (1980) called this variable **power distance**. As a general rule, the more collectivistic a culture is, the greater the power distance. The greater the power distance in a culture, the more the people in power are able to get away with abusing their power. This tempts powerful people in collectivistic cultures to abuse their power especially if they have the opportunity to abuse their power over outgroup members.

These cultural differences have implications on the self-systems of the people in these cultures. Two researchers, Markus and Kitayama (1991) have systematically organized the cognitive, emotional, and motivational implications of these different views of the self. According to Markus and Kitayama (1991), the more individualistic a culture, the more people tend to have an **independent self construal**. The independent self construal is a self-system that predominantly views the individual as separate from others and the environment. Because the individual is considered to be separate from others, having this type of self-system makes us **feel alone** in the world. In contrast, the more collectivistic a culture, the more people tend to have an **interdependent self construal**. The interdependent self construal is a self-system that predominantly views the individual as only a part of a larger group with its members existing in relation to each other. Having this type of self-system makes us feel **less alone** because we see ourselves as part of a group. On the other hand, because we feel like we are a part of a group, we feel **less free** to do whatever we want as individuals. We must cooperate and function in relation to everyone else in the group. In contrast, the people with an independent self construal, feel **more free** to do whatever they want to do because they feel less responsible as a member of anything larger than themselves as individuals.

These differences in the self-systems of the people in these cultures also have important implications on the motivations of these people. As discussed earlier, the main purpose of the self-system is to maintain one's energy level. The more independent our self construal is, the more we try to maintain our energy by taking energy and protecting our energy from others. Thus the more individualistic a culture, the more **competitive** individuals tend to be. Success in individualistic cultures often means being in a position where we can **take more energy than give**. In the United States (an individualistic culture) for example, we want to be a "winner". We want to be more powerful than others. We want to be respected more than others. The more a person with an independent self construal is able to do these things, the more **self-esteem** (i.e., efficient self-system) they tend to have. In contrast, the more interdependent our self construal is, the more we try to maintain our energy by **experiencing unity** with members of our group.

Because of this, people in collectivistic cultures tend to be motivated to **fit in and maintain harmony** with their group. The more a person with an interdependent self construal is able to do these things successfully, the more self-esteem (i.e., efficient self-system) they tend to have. However, as mentioned earlier, people in collectivistic cultures also have the tendency to be more discriminatory toward outgroup members. This implies that a person with an interdependent self construal may be motivated to **take energy from outgroup members** in addition to experiencing unity with ingroup members.

Although geographically not accurate, individualistic cultures are commonly labeled the "**West**" and collectivistic cultures are commonly labeled as the "**East**" or "**non-Western**". In "Western" cultures, people emphasize taking control of things and **making our desires win** over what has, is, or could happen. This tendency has lead to industrialization and technological advance as well as less admirable behaviors such as imperialism in these cultures. In contrast, "non-Western" cultures tend to emphasize unity and harmony by **letting go of our desires** and accepting what has, is, or could happen. This has lead to the development of various famous philosophies and religions that focus on inner peace such as Hinduism, Taoism, and Buddhism, but much less industrialization and technological advance.

Moreover, cross-cultural researchers have suggested that **non-Western** cultures tend to use the **analog** (or **holistic**) mode of functioning more than the digital (or analytical) mode of functioning (Nisbett et al., 2001; Walter, 1994). Their research has revealed that people in these cultures focus more on background information, social contexts, and the larger whole. People in non-Western cultures have more of a tendency to experience things as **subjectively and objectively unified**. Compared to people in Western cultures, they have less of a tendency to separate objects from the subject and objects from other objects. The Chinese Taoist philosophy concerning yin and yang illustrates this tendency very nicely. Taoism maintains that although yang is the foreground and grabs our attention and yin is the background, one cannot exist without the other. The foreground can only exist when there is a background and the background can only exist when there is a foreground. They are both parts of one whole. Prominent philosophies in non-Western cultures such as Taoism, Buddhism, and Hinduism serve as constant reminders about the unity of the universe using clever ways to show us that boundaries are only artificial lines drawn in our minds. Moreover, these philosophies focus on appreciating the present moment rather than focusing on the end result of our behaviors. They are more process-oriented (analog) rather than goal-oriented (digital).

In contrast, Western cultures have more of a tendency to use the **digital** than the analog mode of functioning (Nisbett et al., 2001; Walter, 1994). One of the primary characteristics of the "West" is to objectify our experiences. We **differentiate objects** from the subject as well as objects from objects. This is the basis of scientific analysis and the root of technological advance, one of the outstanding characteristics of the "West". Research in this area has revealed that compared to people in non-Western cultures, people in these cultures tend to pay much more attention to the foreground than the background. In fact, researchers have found that people in Western cultures sometimes focus so much on the foreground information that they often almost completely disregard background information (Nisbett et al., 2001). Consistent with this notion, work in social psychology has also suggested that people in Western cultures focus on the individual (i.e., foreground) and pay minimal attention to social contexts (i.e., background) in their understanding of life events (Markus & Kitayama, 1991; Miller, 1984). Some scholars have also noted that people in the "West" have a tendency to narrow their focus on the object to the extent that they **lose sight of the subject** (e.g., Watts, 1966; Wilber, 1998). When we lose sight of the subject and its relationship with the object, we start seeing ourselves as manipulators of the universe rather than seeing ourselves as participants in the universe.

The Western emphasis on the digital mode of functioning can also be observed in cultural differences in the use of **language**. Although most right-handed people in **Western** cultures predominantly use the **left hemisphere** in processing language, most right-handed people in **non-Western** cultures are known to use **both the left and right cerebral hemispheres** relatively evenly when processing language (Ornstein, 1997). Since the left cerebral hemisphere is largely responsible for digital modes of functioning among most right-handed people, this reflects the high emphasis on the digital mode of functioning among people in Western cultures. Even if we look at the written language of non-Western cultures such as China, we learn that each letter has a certain meaning rather than a certain sound (as in Western language). If we study the evolution of these Chinese letters, we learn that these letters are **ideographic** in nature. Many of these letters are derived from pictures of events and objects that the letter represents. Pictures and visual symbols are primarily processed using the analog mode of functioning. We understand pictures because we relate them to our experiences. We recognize a picture of a dog because we are relating that visual image to our past experiences of seeing a dog. In contrast, the written language of Western cultures is based more on **phonetics**, the sound of the word. For example, in

English, each letter represents a relatively meaningless sound. The digital mode of functioning is largely responsible for differentiating between various sounds.

Evolution and Consciousness

Consciousness is also intricately related to theories of evolution both at the micro and macro level. Evolutionary theory at the micro level is commonly associated with the work of Charles Darwin (1911). According to the theory of evolution at the micro level, **random genetic mutations** occur periodically with all types of organisms. These genetic mutations can cause a variety of physical and psychological changes in the organism. These mutations can range from having longer limbs, stronger jaws, opposable thumbs, sense organs responsive to a wider range of stimuli, to having higher cognitive capacity. Organisms with mutations that are **advantageous for survival and reproduction** are more likely to pass on their genes to the next generation. Organisms with mutations that are disadvantageous for survival and reproduction are less likely to pass on their genes to the next generation. Moreover, when a mutation advantageous for survival and reproduction occurs to an organism, the other organisms without this advantageous mutation are less likely to pass on their genes to the next generation. The theory suggests that through time, any organism that does not have an advantageous genetic make-up (originally caused by a genetic mutation) will become extinct. This is commonly known as the process of **natural selection**.

This implies that, unless there is a genetic mutation in recent generations, every organism alive today has a genetic make-up that is advantageous for survival and reproduction. In other words, we are offspring of generations of organisms who have been successful in surviving and reproducing. Because we are offspring of organisms that have been successful in surviving and reproducing, we have characteristics that are advantageous for our genes to be passed on to the next generation. Moreover, not only do these characteristics help our own survival as individuals, these characteristics also promote the survival and reproduction of our **gene pool**. A gene pool is a term used to characterize organisms that share similar genes. Promoting the survival of our gene pool implies that, for example, we are more likely to promote the survival of our sibling than a distant relative because we share more genes with our siblings than with distant relatives. This theory suggests that if we had a choice to save the life of one of two organisms, we would most likely choose to save the life of the organism that shares more genes with us. This makes us choose to save the lives of our own children over strangers. It makes us humans choose saving the lives of other humans over other animals.

According to this evolutionary approach at the micro level, these psychological tendencies form a large part of our character (Barash, 1982; Wilson, 1975).

Although evolutionary theory at the micro level is focused on genetics and survival of the gene pool, evolutionary theory at the macro level is focused on the evolution of matter. It examines evolution beyond mere physical survival of "living" beings. Let us now turn our focus to this theory at the macro level. Arthur Koestler (1964), one of the originators of systems theory, suggests that matter is organized in a hierarchy ranging from small and simple to large and complex units. Atoms are organized to form molecules, a larger system that forms a whole at the next level. Molecules eventually organize themselves to form an even larger system such as living cells. Living cells are organized to form even larger systems such as multicellular organisms. Multicellular organisms organize to form even larger systems like colonies and tribes. Although I have skipped a few steps in between, this is the basic assumption behind evolutionary theory at the macro level. Koestler calls these systems at each level "**holons**". According to this theory, matter is organized at various levels in a hierarchy of holons. Each holon is made of an organized set of smaller holons. At the same time, however, each holon is or has the potential to become a smaller part of an even larger more complex holon.

According to evolutionary theory at the macro level, matter has evolved into **increasingly larger and more inclusive holons** (i.e., units of energy) ever since the big bang. First we began as small units of matter like atoms and molecules, and then we organized ourselves into living organisms. Finally living individual organisms have organized themselves into even larger units known as colonies and tribes. Humans have come so far as organizing themselves into large groups of people such as nations. As evolution progresses, we will eventually arrive at larger and more inclusive units made of various nations uniting to form a global system of organization. We are beginning to see glimpses of such holons in the last century. The globalization of the world economy as well as the formation of the United Nations may be regarded as beginning signs of such holons.

Just as numerous individuals can unite to form a group through mutual respect and attention, smaller holons at all levels unite to form larger holons through **mutual respect and attention**. Numerous atoms can unite and form a molecule by respecting and paying attention and responding to the needs or desires of each other. Numerous cells can unite and function together as an organism by respecting and paying attention and responding to the needs or desires of each other. Two nations can unite to form a coalition by respecting and paying attention and responding to the needs or desires of each other. This is how evolution progresses. Through mutual respect and attention, we continuously keep forming larger and more inclusive holons. In contrast, if the holons at a lower level are not respectful and attentive to each other, the larger holon disintegrates. If the cells that make up my body do not pay attention and respond to the needs or desires of each other, my body disintegrates and I eventually die. If individuals in a group do not pay attention and respond to the needs or desires of each other, the group disintegrates. Although both the formation of larger holons and the disintegration of holons at all levels are constantly occurring at all times, evolutionary progress continues as long as more of the former occurs than the latter. If there is more of the latter than the former, we will begin moving backwards in our evolution[6].

We learned earlier that self-systems evolve by transcending and including the contents of the former system. In a similar way, holons evolve by transcending and including the contents of the former smaller holons. Thus according to evolutionary theory at the macro level, evolutionary progress is defined as **development of ever-larger holons** through mutual respect and attention. Even within human evolution, we see signs of this type of progress. If we look back at our own history, we can see that there is a significant increase in respect and attention toward the needs and desires of other individuals as well as other groups of individuals. This is evident in the decrease in both the frequency and degree of cruel behaviors such as torture, genocide, war, as well as slavery in the last few centuries. It is also evident in the increase of emphasis on respect for human rights in modern civilizations (e.g., Amnesty International). This increase in respect and attention for others initially lead to the development of tribes. More recently, tribes have organized themselves into larger groups such as nations through mutual respect and attention. In even more recent years, some nations have developed mutual respect and began attending to the each other's desires and needs to form even larger organizations such as the United Nations.

In the previous paragraph, we examined some parallels between the development of the self-system (i.e., human development) and the evolution of holons. In the field of psychology, it was G. Stanley Hall (1904) and his work on **recapitulation theory** that elaborated on the idea that these two processes are highly related to each other. Recapitulation theory states that human development roughly follows the sequence of our evolutionary progress. Even from a purely physical standpoint, this seems true. Evolution has progressed from unicellular organisms (or systems) to multi-cellular organisms. In the same way humans develop from unicellular systems (i.e., sperm and egg) to multi-cellular organisms. In evolution, the first "living" organisms evolved in the ocean. Some of these organisms evolved into fish that require gills to breath in the water. As some of these fish evolved, they developed the ability to live on land. Traces of this process can be witnessed in human prenatal development. During prenatal development, the fetus grows in amniotic fluid that is very similar to the characteristics of water in the ocean. Furthermore, you may also be aware that the human fetus goes through a prenatal stage where we have physical features resembling gills.

In addition to the physical parallels, we can also observe parallels in the psychological aspects of evolution and development. As evolution progresses, we have become more and more attentive and respectful of each other's needs and desires. In the same way, we also learned in earlier sections that as we humans develop, we become less and less egocentric and thus more and more attentive and respectful of each other's needs and desires. Throughout our evolution we have developed the ability to adapt to an increasingly wider variety of situations through the development of culture, technology, intergenerational communication, and natural selection. In a similar way, we also learned in earlier sections that as our self-systems develop we acquire the ability to adapt to an increasingly wider range of situations.

In essence, the more we progress in our evolution, the more we relate to each other as individuals as well as groups with mutual respect and attention. Similarly, the more we progress in our personal development, the more we relate to each other as individuals as well as groups with mutual respect and attention. This implies that the amount of respect we have for others is an indication of where we are in our own personal development. Moreover, where most of us are in our own personal development is a reflection of where we are in the process of evolution. This implies that the more we progress in our personal development as a collective group, the more evolutionary progress we make as a culture of human beings. It takes a critical mass of individuals at an advanced level of personal development for a certain culture to evolve to the next level. Where a certain culture is in the evolutionary process is determined by where the majority of people in that culture are in their personal development. Every culture is at a slightly different point in evolution because the majority of people in those cultures are at slightly different stages in their personal development (Beck & Cowan, 1996).

Historical Development of Theory

While we are discussing the evolution of culture, let us briefly examine recent historical developments of western civilization in the understanding of nature. Before the **enlightenment period** (17th-19th century), the Church was the primary source of "truth", our understanding of nature. At this point in history, the church was extremely powerful. The pope, priests and other religious figures largely determined what was true, what is good, and what the meaning of life is. During the enlightenment period (17th-19th century), people began questioning the ideas put forth by the church and various people began suggesting that we should rely less on the church and more on empirical observations to understand nature (e.g., Descartes, 1956; Leibnitz, 1982; Newton, 1964). This gave rise to an emphasis on investigations of nature using empirical observations (i.e., things we can clearly see). Due to this emphasis on empirical observations, people began relying more and more on objective reality rather than spiritual and moral messages from the church to understand the "truth". During this period, more and more people began to consider objective reality as the absolute truth. Furthermore, because empirical observation is the basis for most natural sciences, this movement facilitated the rapid development of the natural sciences. This development of the natural sciences contributed to industrialization as well as the many technological and medical advances we see today.

During the twentieth century, various scholars began questioning the existence of objective reality (e.g., Foucault, 1994; Derrida, 1998). This signified the beginning of a movement that we now call **post-modernism**. Various post-modernist scholars turned our attention to the limitations of traditional natural sciences by discovering that there is no such thing as completely objective or absolute reality. These scholars of consciousness reminded us of the idea that everything is subjective to some extent. They suggested that the mere act of a person observing an object makes that experience subjective because the object is perceived in relation to that particular person. If someone else were to observe the same object, he or she would perceive it in relation to his or her own self and therefore the experience would never be the same as the experience of the former person observing the object. These theorists claim that we can only see things through our own self-systems and since everyone has a different self-system, everyone sees things differently.

This focus on the subjectivity of our experiences has lead to the emphasis on social contexts in understanding various aspects of nature. Because our experiences are subjective, we must consider the social context (i.e., how the observer is relating to the object) to develop a better understanding of things. This emphasis is most noticeable in a post-modern movement known as **social constructionism**. Social constructionism claims that things have no meaning without its social context. Therefore, what may be considered to be true in one context may not be considered true in another. For example, winking at an acquaintance at a social event may be interpreted as flirting while winking at an ally in a hostile combat situation may be interpreted as a sign that we have a secret plan. Moreover, what may be considered to be good in one context may not be considered good in another. For instance, suicide simply as an escape from life may be considered unacceptable even though suicide to save the lives of fifty others may be considered acceptable. Social constructionists claim that we must consider the social context of everything we study in order to truly understand things.

Cultural relativism, a concept based on the assumptions of social contructionism, is an application of these ideas to cultural differences in moral values. Cultural relativism refers to the idea that all moral values are based on unique cultural contexts. It suggests that we must always consider the cultural context before we make any moral judgments about any behavior or event. This means that what may be considered to be morally correct in one culture may not be morally correct in another. Although this seems reasonable at first glance, this idea can lead to severe implications if taken to its extreme. It implies that people outside of a certain culture (and thus do not fully understand the cultural context) have very little basis to determine whether something is morally correct in another culture. Thus we have no right to condemn people in other cultures for doing something that would be morally wrong from our own cultural perspective. According to this perspective, even extreme behaviors like mass genocide, torture, spousal abuse, and child abuse may be considered to be acceptable given certain unique cultural circumstances incomprehensible to most outsiders.

Some scholars have taken this idea even one step further and have stated that there is no absolute meaning to anything at all because everything depends on how it relates to everything else (e.g., social context, culture, etc.). According to this view, there is no such thing as absolute truth and there are no moral laws or values that are universal. Everything is relative. This perspective is often referred to as **radical cultural relativism**.

In sum, we could characterize the enlightenment as a move from subjectivity to objectivity and post-modernism as a move from objectivity to a new type of objectivity that accounts for the subjectivity of our perceptions. As is evident from the descriptions above, both of these extremes (i.e., overemphasis on objective reality and overemphasis on the subjectivity of our experiences) lead to limitations in our pursuit to our understanding of nature. Unfortunately this separation between the subjective and objective approaches to understanding, however, is the root of the separation between the arts (or humanities) and the natural sciences that we still see today. Although it may not be noticeable to us at first glance, this situation is gradually changing in the recent centuries. Recent approaches to our understanding of nature such as the theories of relativity, chaos theory, quantum theory, systems theory, transpersonal theory, and string theory have suggested an integration of both of these approaches. Many of these approaches integrate the study of our own consciousness (i.e., subjectivity) with the study of objective reality in order to arrive at a more complete understanding of nature (e.g., Beck & Cowan, 1996; Capra, 2000; Koestler, 1964; Wilber, 1995). In essence these fields of inquiry are integrating the approaches traditionally used in the arts (or humanities) and the natural sciences to develop a more complete understanding of nature. Through their work, many of these scholars are suggesting that although we are participants of the evolutionary process, we are not the ones "making" it happen. It is something that is happening and we can learn to accept and facilitate the process by participating in it or we can frustrate ourselves by resisting our participation and trying to control the process.

Many of these scholars are also responsible for developing evolutionary theory at the macro level (e.g., Koestler, 1964; Wilber, 1995). They suggest that evolution does not merely occur by random mutations and natural selection. They suggest that evolution has a specific direction. As discussed earlier, through the development of mutual respect and attention, evolution is moving toward the development of increasingly larger and more inclusive holons. This idea has an important implication on our values and morality. Since we regard evolutionary progress as the formation of larger holons through mutual respect and attention, anything that facilitates this process is valued highly and commonly considered as morally correct. On the other hand, since evolutionary regression is regarded as the disintegration of holons from a lack of mutual respect and attention, anything that facilitates this process is valued much less and commonly considered as morally wrong.

As you may recall from an earlier discussion of Piaget and Inhelder's (1969) work, we move through various levels of consciousness during our development. Just as G. Stanley Hall (1904) suggested with his recapitulation theory, it is evident that these developments in consciousness parallel the evolutionary progress we have made. During the enlightenment period, a large number of people began moving from consciousness at level 1 to level 2 by objectifying our experiences. The movement that we call post-modernism is representative of the move from consciousness at level 2 to consciousness at level 3. At this point, many of us began thinking about our own thinking and began increasing our awareness of how our own consciousness influences our perception of the "objective" world around us. The most recent movement beyond post-modernism that integrates the subjective with the objective perspective can be considered as the move from consciousness at level 3 to consciousness at level 4. At this point, some people have developed their consciousness to the point that they are able to consciously think about themselves thinking about how our seemingly "objective" thoughts and perceptions are partly subjective.

Conclusions

Many things have been discussed and it is difficult to figure out a reasonable way to put it all together. In order to conclude, I will just note what I feel is important to remember in our everyday lives using a variety of well-known proverbs from Native American tribes. First let's begin with a general message about the rhythm of nature. The Cheyenne native tribe has a proverb that translates, "When you lose the rhythm of the drumbeat of God, you are lost from the peace and rhythm of life." In nature, holons at every level are constantly giving and receiving in a rhythmic fashion. Regardless of our culture, we as humans must remember to recognize and participate in this rhythm of giving and receiving. Although culture guides the process of giving and receiving through scripts, we cannot solely rely on culture. Our happiness is perhaps highly related to our ability to dance to this rhythm. In order to stay in synchrony with this rhythm, it is most important to always remember that we need to give in addition to receive (since we never forget to take). The Arapaho native tribe has a proverb that translates, "When we show our respect for other living things, they respond with respect for us." This emphasizes this idea. As a general rule, the more we give the more we receive. In order to give, we need to let go of our own selfish desires and be respectful and pay attention to the many people and things around us. We need to be a good listener. We need to think about how others feel. We need to put our selves in the positions of others before we do things, make judgments, or make decisions. The Huron native tribe has a proverb that translates, "Listen to the voice of nature for it holds treasures for you." There is beauty in everything if we look close enough. There is something positive in everything and everyone. There is something positive in every experience. There is something to be thankful for in every situation. The Minquass native tribe has a proverb that translates, "If you see no reason for giving thanks, the fault lies in yourself." If we are able to find and appreciate these treasures, we will always be able stay with the waves of life and never stray too much from the beautiful rhythm of nature.

In order to do this successfully, we need to remind ourselves never to take power for granted, regardless of whether it is physical or social. The Seneca native tribe has a proverb that translates, "He who has great power should use it lightly." When we are in a position of social power, we are not only tempted to steal energy but we often do steal energy from others without conscious awareness. This is why many people say, "Lead by example." The Sioux native tribe has a proverb that translates, "Do not point the way, but lead the way." When we tell other people what to do, we take or sometimes even steal their energy. When we lead people by doing what we want others to do ourselves, we inspire them. Although we all tend to believe that being strong and tough is having the ability to overpower others and make others do things by force, as the Iroquois native proverb states, "The greatest strength is gentleness." Real toughness is not the ability to overpower and dominate but the ability to remain in unity with the environment regardless of what happens. This is how extraordinary people, regardless of culture, are able to behave gracefully in many difficult situations. They remain calm, composed, attentive, and respectful even in the most threatening types of situations. As a general rule, the calmer we are, the more we are able to pay attention to a wider range of phenomena and the longer our attention span (Goleman, 1985). This enables us to be more patient as well as respectful and attentive of the needs and desires of a wider range of holons in nature (including other people).

Lastly, it may be useful to remind our selves of an insightful native proverb by the Lakota native tribe that translates, "Creation is ongoing." Evolutionary, social, and personal development is ongoing and involves the formation of ever larger and more encompassing holons through mutual attention and respect. With industrialization and modernization of cultures, we humans are beginning to regard ourselves more and more as controllers of this process rather than participants in the process. As some scholars have noted, it is evident that this change in perspective has lead to many of our present social, environmental, and political problems (e.g., Capra, 1982; Wilber, 1998). It is crucial to remember that we ourselves are holons, are made of smaller holons, and are also parts of much larger holons. Thus we must begin regarding ourselves more as participants in this process rather than controllers of this process.

I sincerely hope that this journey has been enjoyable and interesting to you. Thank you very much for your attention and interest. It is a true blessing to have the opportunity to think and write about these things. I also feel very blessed to have the opportunity to participate in the dialogue of developing an understanding of nature (including ourselves) with so many insightful individuals throughout my life. I wish you all the best of luck for the development of your own self-systems and would be delighted if anything in this book has helped in that process.

References

Adler, A. (1954). *Understanding human nature*. New York: Fawcett books.

Ainsworth, M. D. S. (1979). Infant-mother attachment. *American Psychologist, 34*, 932-937.

Ainsworth, M. D. S., Blehar, M. C., Waters, E., & Wall, S. (1978). *Patterns of attachment*. Hillsdale, NJ: Erlbaum.

Bakan, D. (1966). *The duality of human existence: An essay on psychology and religion*. Chicago, IL: Rand McNally.

Banks, M. S. (1980). The development of visual accomodation during early infancy, *Child Development, 51*, 646-666.

Barash, D. P. (1982). *Sociobiology and behavior* (2nd ed.). New York: Elsevier.

Baumeister, R. F., Muraven, M. & Tice, D. M. (2000). Ego depletion: A resource model of volition, self-regulation, and controlled processing. *Social Cognition, 18*, 130-150.

Baumrind, D. (1971). Current patterns of parental authority. *Developmental Psychology Monograph, 4*, (No. 1, Pt. 2).

Beattie, M. (1997). *Codependent no more* (2nd ed.). Center City, MN: Hazelden.

Beck, D. E., & Cowan, C. C. (1996). *Spiral dynamics: Mastering values, leadership, and change*. Oxford, UK: Blackwell.

Berne, E. (1964). *Games people play*. New York: Random House.

Black Elk, W., & Lyon, W. S. (1991). *Black Elk: The sacred ways of Lakota*. San Francisco, CA: Harper San Francisco.

Bornstein, R. F. (1989). Exposure and affect: Overview and meta-analysis of research, 1968-1978. *Psychological Bulletin, 106*, 265-289.

Bornstein, R. F., & D'Agostino, P. R. (1992). Stimulus recognition and the mere exposure effect. *Journal of Personality and Social Psychology, 63*, 545-552.

Brewer, M. B. (1991). The social self: On being the same and different at the same time. *Personality and Social Psychology Bulletin, 17*, 475-482.

Brewer, M. B. (2001). The social self: On being the same and different at the same time. In M. A. Hogg (Ed.), *Intergroup relations: Essential readings* (pp. 245-253). Philadelphia, PA: Psychology Press.

Byrne, D. (1971). *The attraction paradigm*. New York: Academic Press.

Capra, F. (2000). *The tao of physics: An exploration of the parallels between modern physics and eastern mysticism* (4th ed.). Boston: Shambhala.

Capra, F. (1982). *The turning point: Science, society and the rising culture*. New York: Simon & Schuster.

Csikszentmihalyi, M. (1991). *Flow: The psychology of optimal experience*. New York: HarperCollins.

Darwin, C. (1911). *The origin of species*. London, UK: John Murray. (Original work published 1859).

Derrida, J. (1998). *Monolingualism of the other: Or, the prosthesis of origin* (trans. P. Mensah). Stanford, CA: Stanford University Press.

Descartes, R. (1956). *Discourse on method* (trans. L. J. Lafleur). Indianapolis: Bobbs-Merrill. (Original work published 1637).

Erikson, E. H. (1963). *Childhood and society* (2nd ed.). New York: Norton.

Erikson, E. H. (1968). *Identity, youth, and crisis*. New York: Norton.

Erikson, E. H. (1978). *Adulthood*. New York: Norton.

Fairbairn, W. R. D. (1974). *Psychoanalytic studies of the personality*. New York: Routledge.

Festinger, L. (1957). *A theory of cognitive dissonance*. Stanford, CA: Stanford University Press.

Foucault, M. (1994). *The order of things: An archeology of the human sciences* (2nd e.). New York: Vintage Books.

Freud, S. (1966). *The complete introductory lectures on psychoanalysis.* (trans. J. Strachey). New York: Norton.

Fromm, E. (1941). *Escape from freedom.* New York: Rinehart.

Gazzinaga, M. S. (1995). Consciousness and the cerebral hemispheres. In M. S. Gazzinaga (Ed.), *The cognitive neurosciences.* Cambridge, MA: MIT Press.

Gilligan, C. (1982). *In a different voice: Psychological theory of women's development.* Cambridge, MA: Harvard University Press.

Goffman, E. (1974). *Frame Analysis.* Cambridge, MA: Harvard University Press.

Goleman, D. (1985). *Vital lies, simple truths: The psychology of self-deception.* New York: Simon & Schuster.

Goleman, D. (1995). *Emotional intelligence: Why it can matter more than IQ for character, health and lifelong achievement.* New York: Bantam Books.

Gottman, J. (1995). *Why marriages succeed or fail: And how you can make yours last.* New York: Fireside.

Guntrip, H. (1964). *Personality structure and human interaction: The developing synthesis of psychodynamic theory.* New York: International University Press.

Hall, G. S. (1904). *Adolescence: Its psychology and its relation to physiology, anthropology, sociology, sex, crime, religion and education* (Vols. 1 and 2). New York: Appleton.

Hazan, C., & Shaver, P. R. (1987). Romantic love conceptualized as an attachment process. *Journal of Personality and Social Psychology, 52,* 511-524.

Heider, F. (1958). *The psychology of interpersonal relations.* New York: John Wiley & Sons.

Hofstede, G. (1980). *Culture's consequences: Comparing values, behaviours, institutions and organizations across nations.* Beverly Hills, CA: Sage Publications.

Hogg, M. A., (1992). *The social psychology of group cohesiveness: From attraction to social identity.* London, UK: Harvester Wheatsheaf.

Janis, I. L. (1982). *Groupthink: Psychological studies of policy decisions and fiascoes.* Boston: Houghton Mifflin.

Jung, C. G. (1936). *The archetypes and the collective unconscious* (Collected works of C. G. Jung, Vol. 9, Pt. 1). London, UK: Routledge.

Jung, C. G. (1958). *The undiscovered self.* London, UK: Routledge.

Katherine, A. (1993). *Boundaries: Where you end and I begin.* New York: Fireside.

Kimura, D. (1999). *Sex and cognition.* Cambridge, MA: MIT Press.

Koestler, A. (1964). *The act of creation.* New York: Dell.

Kohlberg, L. (1981). *The philosophy of moral development: Essays on moral development* (vol. 1). San Francisco: Harper & Row.

Kübler-Ross, E. (1969). *On death and dying.* New York: Macmillan.

Kübler-Ross, E. (1975). *Death: The final stage of growth.* Englewood Cliffs, NJ: Prentice-Hall.

Leary, T. F. (1955). The theory and measurement methodology of interpersonal communication. *Psychiatry, 18,* 147-161.

Leary, T. F. (1957). *Interpersonal diagnosis of personality.* New York: Ronald.

Leibniz, G. W. (1982). *New essays on human understanding* (ed. & trans. P. Remnant & J. Bennett). Cambridge, MA: Cambridge University Press. (Original work published in 1765).

Levinson, D. (1978). *Seasons of a man's life.* New York: Knopf.

Luborsky, L. (1984). *Principles of psychoanalytic psychotherapy: A manual for Supportive-Expressive Treatment.* New York: Basic Books.

Mahler M. S. (1968). *On human symbiosis and the vicissitudes of individuation: Infantile psychosis.* New York: International Universities Press.

Main, M., & Solomon, J. (1986). Discovery of an insecure disorganized / disoriented attachment pattern: Procedures, findings and implications for classification of behavior. In M. Yogman, & T. B. Brazelton (Eds.), *Affective development in infancy* (pp. 95-124). Norwood, NJ: Ablex.

Main, M., & Weston, D. R. (1981). The quality of the toddler's relationship to mother and father: Related to conflict behavior and readiness to establish new relationships. *Child Development, 52,* 932-940.

Markus, H. R., & Kitayama, S. (1991). Culture and the self: Implications for cognition, emotion, and motivation. *Psychological Review, 98,* 224-253.

Maslow, A. H. (1970). *Motivation and personality* (2nd ed.). New York: Harper and Row.

McAdams, D. P. (1985). *Power, intimacy and the life story: Personological inquiries into identity.* Homewood, IL: Dorsey Press.

Medvec, V. H., Madey, S. F., & Gilovich, T. (1995). When less is more: Counterfactual thinking and satisfaction among Olympic medallists. *Journal of Personality and Social Psychology, 72,* 1284-1296.

Mellody, P. (1989). *Facing Codependence: What it is, where it comes from, how it sabotages our lives.* San Francisco, CA: Harper San Francisco.

Mesquita, B., & Frijda, N. H. (1992). Cultural variations in emotions: A review. *Psychological Bulletin, 112,* 179-204.

Miller, J. G. (1984). Culture and development of everyday social explanation. *Journal of Personality and Social Psychology, 46,* 961-978.

Newton, I. (1964). *The mathematical principles of natural philosophy.* New York: Citadel Press. (Original work published 1687).

Nisbett, R. E., Peng, K., Choi, I. Norenzayan, A. (2001). Culture and systems of thought: Holistic versus analytic cognition. *Psychological Review, 108,* 291-310.

Ornstein, R. (1997). *The right mind: Making sense of the hemispheres.* New York Harcourt.

Osgoode, C. E. (1962). *An alternative to war or surrender.* Urbana, IL: University of Illinois Press.

Piaget, J. (1973). *To understand is to invent.* New York: Grossman.

Piaget, J., & Inhelder, B. (1969). *The psychology of the child.* New York: Basic books.

Redfield, J. (1993). *The celestine prophecy.* New York: Warner.

Rogers, C. R. (1951). *Client-centered therapy: Its current practice, implications, and theory.* Boston, Houghton Mifflin.

Rogers, C. R. (1959). A theory of therapy, personality and interpersonal relationships, as developed in the client centered framework. In S. Koch (Ed.), *Psychology: A study of a science* (vol. 3). New York: McGraw-Hill.

Rogers, C. R. (1961). *On becoming a person.* Boston: Houghton Mifflin.

Rubin, J. Z., Pruitt, D. G., & Kim, S. H. (1994). *Social conflict: Escalation, stalemate, and settlement.* New York: McGraw-Hill.

Sartre, J-P. (1957). *The transcendence of the ego.* (trans. F. Williams & R. Kirkpatrick). New York: Noonday Press.

Sato, T. (1998). Agency and communion: The relationship between therapy and culture. *Cultural Diversity and Mental Health, 4,* 278-290.

Sato, T. (2001). Autonomy and relatedness in psychopathology and treatment: A cross-cultural formulation. *Genetic, Social, and General Psychology Monographs, 127,* 89-127.

Sato, T. (2003). *Rhythm, relationships, and transcendence: Patterns in the complex web of life.* Lincoln, Nebraska: Writers Club Press.

Sato, T., Slacum, K. M., McGoff, E. P., & Murray, C. A. (2003, March). *Introversion-extraversion and muscial/artistic preference.* Paper presented at the 2003 annual convention of the Eastern Psychological Association, Baltimore, Maryland, USA.

Saunders, J. B. (1989). The efficacy of treatment for drinking problems. Special issue: Psychiatry and the addictions. *International Review of Psychiatry, 1*, 121-137.

Seligman, M. E. P. (1991). *Learned optimism.* New York: Knopf.

Schank, R. C., & Abelson, R. P. (1977). *Scripts, plans, goals and understanding: An inquiry into human knowledge structures.* Hillsdale, NJ: Lawrence Erlbaum and Associates.

Sullivan, H. S. (1953). *Interpersonal theory of psychiatry.* New York: Norton.

Strupp, H. H., & Binder, J. L. (1984). *Psychotherapy in a new key: A guide to Time-Limited Dynamic Psychotherapy.* New York: Basic Books.

Szasz, T. (1961). *The myth of mental illness.* New York: Harper & Row.

Tajfel, H. (1981). *Human groups and social categories: Studies in social psychology.* London: Cambridge University Press.

Ting-Toomey, S. (1998). *Communicating across cultures.* New York: Guilford Press.

Triandis, H. C. (1995). *Individualism and collectivism.* Boulder, CO: Westview Press.

Turner, J. C. (1987). *Rediscovering the social group: A self-categorization theory.* New York: Basil Blackwell.

Walter, K. (1994). *Tao of Chaos: Merging east and west.* Rockport, MA: Element books.

Watts, A. (1966). *The book: On the taboo against knowing who you are.* New York: Vintage books.

Watzlawick, P., Beavin, J. H., & Jackson, D. D. (1967). *Pragmatics of human communication: A study of interactional patterns, pathologies, and paradoxes.* New York: Norton.

Watzlawick, P. Weakland, J., & Fisch, M. D. (1974). *Change: Principles of problem formation and problem resolution.* New York: Norton.

Whitfield, C. L. (1993). *Boundaries and relationships: Knowing, protecting, and enjoying the self.* Deerfield Beach, FL: Health Communications.

Wilber, K. (1970). *No Boundary: Eastern and Western approaches to personal growth.* Boston: Shambala.

Wilber, K. (1995). *Sex, ecology, and spirituality: The spirit of evolution.* Boston: Shambala.

Wilber, K. (1998). *The eye of spirit: An integral vision for a world gone slightly mad.* Boston: Shambala.

Wilson, E. O. (1975). *Sociobiology: The new synthesis.* Cambridge, MA: Harvard University Press.

Wilson, E. O. (1998). *Consilience: The unity of knowledge.* New York: Knopf.

Wortman, C., & Silver, R. (1989). The myths of coping with loss. *The Journal of Consulting and Clinical Psychology, 57,* 349-357.

Endnotes

[1] Figure A is a diagram displaying the range of experiences that we as individuals can have with particular other individuals at any given moment. Any social experience can be placed somewhere in this two dimensional space. The right end of the horizontal dimension represents unity or a sense of togetherness and the left end represents separation or a sense of detachment. The upper half of the vertical dimension represents dominance or a sense of control. The level on this side of the dimension represents how much energy we are receiving. The more dominant, controlling, and influential we feel, the more energy we receive. The bottom half of the vertical dimension represents submission or a sense of being influenced or controlled. The level on this side of the dimension represents how much energy we are giving away. The more we feel like we are influenced or controlled by others, the more energy we give away.

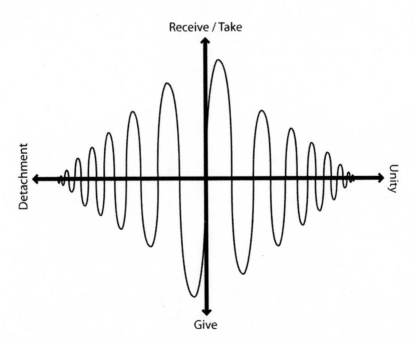

Figure A. Spectrum of Relationship Experiences

The waves in Figure A represent the rhythmic nature of our experiences of giving and receiving. They also provide a general indication of the emotional stability experienced at each point on the horizontal dimension. The smaller the waves, the more emotionally stable. The waves suggest that the more togetherness and unity we experience with the other person, the more emotionally stable we feel. This is why we use the expression, "Things are fine" when our relationships are stable. In contrast, the more dominant or submissive one feels toward the other person the more emotionally unstable we feel (either positively of negatively aroused) and thus the waves go up and down more radically. In these situations, we typically feel highly dominant in one moment and then we feel highly dominated in the next moment. This is why we commonly say that, "things are rough" when we are not getting along well with someone. If we turn to the other end of the horizontal dimension, we notice that the waves become smaller as we detach ourselves from others. The more detached we are from someone, the less unstable we feel regarding that particular relationship. We feel less unstable because that particular relationship does not concern us at the time. It should be noted here that detachment is not a general experience in itself. We are usually detached from someone because we are focusing on a relationship with something or someone else at the time and not on the relationship with the person we are detached from. This implies that the left side of the horizontal dimension corresponds to the relationships we have with things that we are not directly engaged with. This side of the horizontal dimension considers the fact that we are simultaneously embedded in many relationships. For example, I may have a relationship with my son and a relationship with my spouse among many others. Let's take these two relationships as a simple example to explain the concept of detachment. When I am at home and interacting with my spouse in the kitchen while my son is in his room playing his guitar with his friend, I am relating to my spouse more than I am relating to my son. Therefore, I am on the right side of the horizontal axis in terms of my relationship with my spouse but on the left side of the horizontal axis in terms of my relationship with my son. While I am interacting with my spouse in this case, I still may be interacting with my son in a remote way. For example, I may care about what he is doing and may pay some peripheral attention to his guitar sounds from the kitchen. In this way, I am slightly attending to my son's behavior and my experience of those moments is slightly influenced by my son's behavior. My son may also care about my presence in the house and hear me speaking to my spouse from his room even though he may not be paying much attention to what exactly I am saying. In a sense, my son is slightly attending to my behavior and his experience of those moments is slightly influenced by my behavior. In this case, my son and I are relatively detached from each other because both of us are attending to something other than each other more intensely. In my case this something other is my spouse. In my son's case it may be his friend who is visiting him.

The less attention my son and I pay to each other, the less we influence each other and the more detached we are from each other and the further left we move on the horizontal axis. However, the less attention we pay to each other, the more attention we are paying to someone or something else. We only fail to pay attention to something when we are attending to something else more. This is how attention works. We cannot pay attention to absolutely nothing just as we cannot pay attention to absolutely everything. Thus complete detachment with something means complete unity with something else. They are both the same state of mind.

[2] Although this analogy of the connectedness of matter facilitates our understanding of the connectedness of all things, it should not be taken literally since there is also a connection between matter and absence of matter.

[3] When the shells around the self-system are so thin that it disappears, we have reached a state of complete transcendence. When we reach this state, we have no self-system. There is no self-system to protect and be defensive about. Because we do not differentiate (our selves from others, one situation from another) in this state, we are in unity with everything (see Figure B).

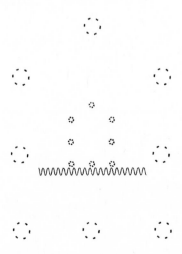

Figure B. Self-System of a Person Experiencing Complete Transcendence

[4] Therefore, the forceful way to help others grow involves a two-step process. The first is taking energy (i.e., breaking down the self-system) from the other person and the second is to open up and share energy (i.e., provide emotional support) with the other person. Figure C is a diagram using the ocean analogy to illustrate the two steps.

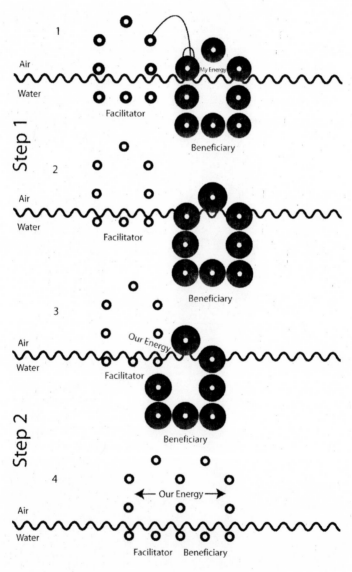

Figure C. The Forceful Way to Help Others Grow

[5] Although it is sometimes more time-consuming, the patient way only involves the second step in the two-step process discussed in the forceful way (see Figure C).

[6] As is evident from this explanation, holons at any level have two general tendencies. The first is a tendency for self-preservation. It is the tendency to keep all of its parts together so that it can continue to function as a whole. This tendency is associated with the digital mode of functioning. It makes us conscious of ourselves as separate individuals and motivates us to protect ourselves from disintegrating into smaller holons. The other tendency of all holons is to integrate itself into a larger whole. This is the tendency to unite with other holons to form even larger holons. This tendency is associated with the analog mode of functioning. It makes us conscious of ourselves as parts of larger holons and motivates us to harmoniously unite with others so that we can function efficiently as larger holons.

0-595-29004-3